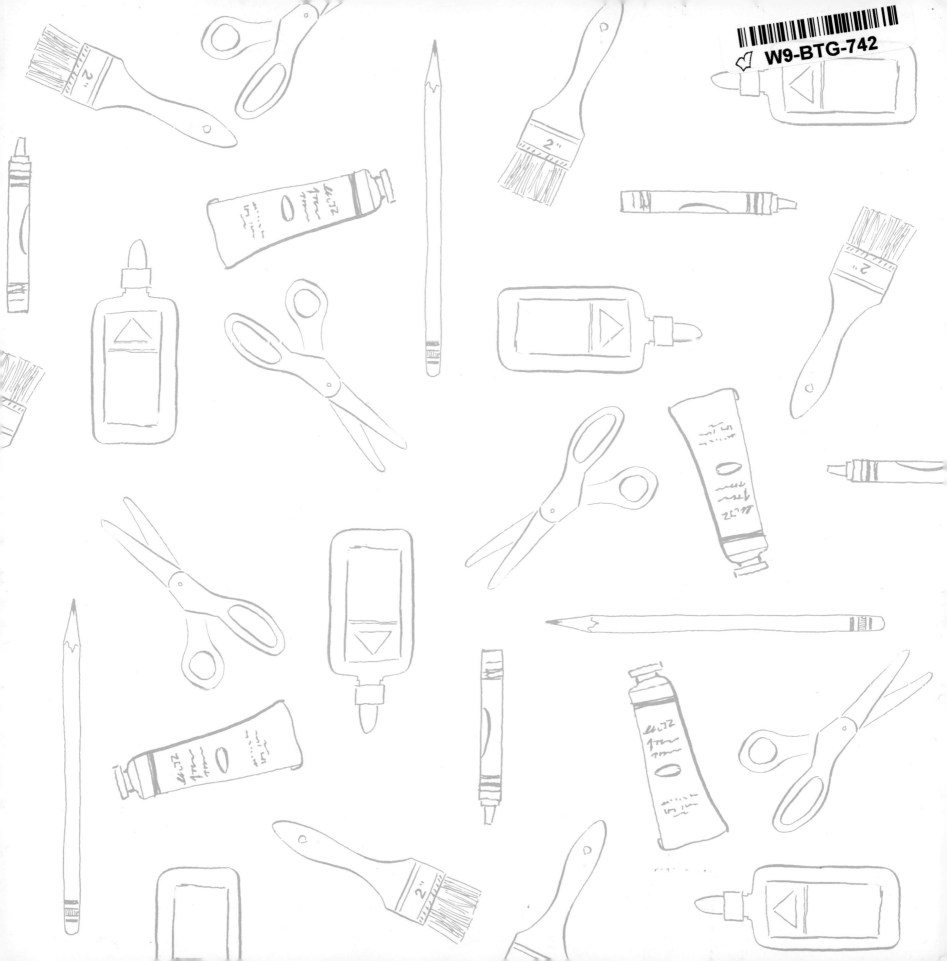

A CHILD'S INTRODUCTION TO

ART

A CHILD'S INTRODUCTION TO
ART

The World's Greatest Paintings and Sculptures

· · · · · · · · · · · · · · · · · · · ·

By HEATHER ALEXANDER

ILLUSTRATED BY MEREDITH HAMILTON

BLACK DOG
& LEVENTHAL
PUBLISHERS
NEW YORK

Photo and Art Credits:

Pages 10, 63
Gianni Dagli Orti/The Art Archive at Art Resource, NY

Pages 11, 12, 23, 25, 26, 31, 33, 39, 43, 49, 51, 67, 69
Erich Lessing/Art Resource, NY

Page 11
© istock.com/pius99

Page 14, top right
© istock.com/david5962

Page 15
© istock.com/RobLopshire (far left)
© istock.com/upsidedowndog (left)
© istock.com/lokapik (top right)
© istock.com/edurivero (bottom right)

Pages 13, 45, 53
Album/Art Resource, NY

Pages 14, 29, 41, 55
© The Metropolitan Museum of Art. Image source: Art Resource, NY

Page 17
© RMN-Grand Palais/Art Resource, NY

Pages 19, 61
© National Gallery, London/Art Resource, NY

Page 21
Alfredo Dagli Orti/The Art Archive at Art Resource, NY

Page 34
Scala/Art Resource, NY
Page 47
The Philadelphia Museum of Art/Art Resource, NY

Page 59
© Vanni Archive/Art Resource, NY

Pages 65, 83, 85
© The Museum of Modern Art/Licensed by SCALA/Art Resource, NY

Page 71
© 2014 The Munch Museum/The Munch-Ellingsen Group/Artists Rights Society (ARS), NY. Image source: Erich Lessing/Art Resource, NY

Page 73
CCI/The Art Archive at Art Resource, NY

Page 77
© 2014 Succession H. Matisse/Artists Rights Society (ARS), New York
Image source: © The Museum of Modern Art/Licensed by SCALA/Art Resource, NY

Page 79
© 2014 Artists Rights Society (ARS), New York
Image source: Erich Lessing/Art Resource, NY

Page 81
Snark/Art Resource, NY

Pg 83
© 2014 Estate of Pablo Picasso/Artists Rights Society (ARS), New York. Image source: © The Museum of Modern Art/Licensed by SCALA/Art Resource, NY

Pg 87
© 2014 The Pollock-Krasner Foundation/Artists Rights Society (ARS), New York
Image source: © The Museum of Modern Art/Licensed by SCALA/Art Resource, NY

Page 89
© 2014 The Jacob and Gwendolyn Lawrence Foundation, Seattle/Artists Rights Society (ARS), New York
Image source: © The Museum of Modern Art/Licensed by SCALA/Art Resource, NY

Page 91
© 2014 The Andy Warhol Foundation for the Visual Arts, Inc. / Artists Rights Society (ARS), New York. Image source: © 2014 Museum Associates/LACMA. Licensed by Art Resource, NY

Published by
Black Dog & Leventhal Publishers, Inc.
151 West 19th Street
New York, NY 10011

Distributed by
Workman Publishing Company
225 Varick Street
New York, NY 10014

Manufactured in China

Cover and interior design by Sheila Hart Design

ISBN-13: 978-1-57912-956-9

h g f e d c b a

Library of Congress Cataloging-in-Publication Data

For my mom, who introduced me to the NYC art museums
—H. A.

With thanks to Peter L. who kindly lets me paint in his barn.
—M. H.

Contents

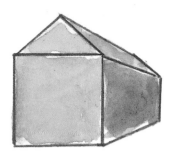

Let's Talk Art

"A man climbs a mountain because it is there.
A man makes a work of art because it is not there."
—SCULPTOR CARL ANDRE

What is art?

Art is not one thing. Art is all around you—from the doodles on your homework papers to the painting in your living room to the family photos you took during the holidays. In this book, we focus on famous paintings, drawings, and sculptures. However, visual art also includes collage, stained glass, photography, printmaking, graffiti, movie posters, advertising, design, and probably many other things we've missed.

What's the point?

Most artists will answer that art makes them happy. They are happy when they make it. They are happy when they look at it.

But art is more than fun and decoration. Art is a way to express yourself. You can tell a story or record

what someone looks like. You can share your feelings or communicate ideas or opinions. You can even take a closer look at the world and explore your dreams and nightmares.

Where is art?

Everywhere. The art in this book is mostly found in museums, but art can be displayed in public buildings, churches, theaters, parks, on the sides of buildings, and even throughout your school. Look and see all the art that surrounds you.

Do you see what I see?

Is *looking* at art the same as *seeing* art? You use your eyes to look at art, and your eyes send the image to your brain. But your brain tells you what to see depending on your age, your interests, your experience, and how you are feeling that day.

For example, look up at the clouds. What shapes and figures do the clouds make? What you see and what your friend sees may not be the same. Just like with clouds, people often view the same piece of art differently. There is no right or wrong when viewing art. Different is just different. Love it or hate it, good art makes us think.

What is an art style?

This book looks at 35 artists. Every artist has his or her own **style**. A style is like a signature. In this book, you will see a bunch of terms that end in "**ism**." These terms describe a style of art or a **movement**. A movement is when lots of artists begin to paint or create in a similar style.

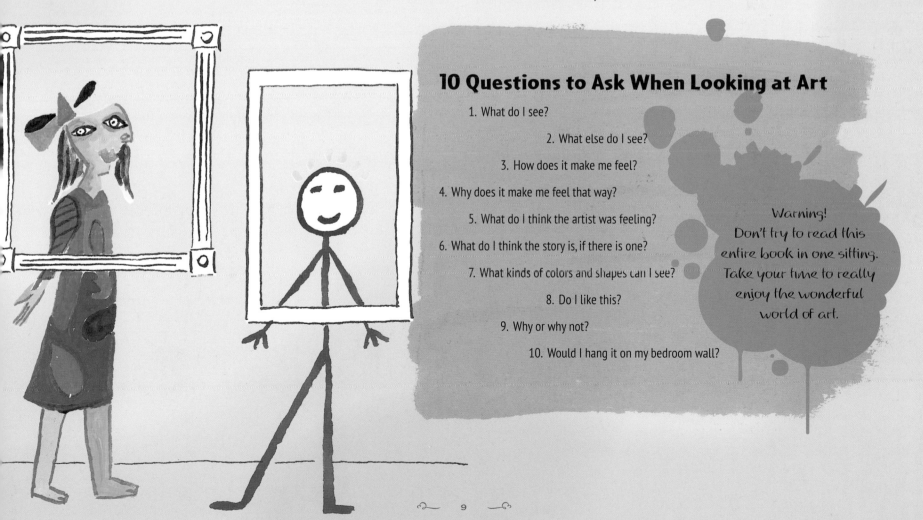

10 Questions to Ask When Looking at Art

1. What do I see?

2. What else do I see?

3. How does it make me feel?

4. Why does it make me feel that way?

5. What do I think the artist was feeling?

6. What do I think the story is, if there is one?

7. What kinds of colors and shapes can I see?

8. Do I like this?

9. Why or why not?

10. Would I hang it on my bedroom wall?

Warning!
Don't try to read this entire book in one sitting. Take your time to really enjoy the wonderful world of art.

IN THE BEGINNING . . .

No one knows when humans first began to draw. The earliest paintings have been found on walls deep inside caves and date as far back as 30,000 B.C. During this time, people hunted for and gathered their food. They moved from place to place, following the animals, and they made their tools from stone, bone, or wood. No metals were used, so this time is called the Stone Age.

Cave Paintings at Lascaux
(ABOUT 18,000 B.C., LASCAUX, FRANCE)

In 1940, four boys in Lascaux, France, took their dog for a walk. The area was filled with limestone caves. Their dog scampered off and disappeared down a hole, and the boys crawled in after him. They found themselves in a large underground space. One boy lit a match and, in the flickering light, they saw an amazing sight. The walls and ceiling were covered with primitive paintings of animals! The next day they told their teacher and returned with a lamp to better see the cave paintings. The caves contained more than 600 paintings and 1,500 engravings. Art historians figured out that these images were painted about nearly 20,000 years ago.

The images were mostly of moving animals—bison, bulls, deer, and horses—that were hunted in this area of France. Some people believe the art was made to help people hunt. Others believe they were made to tell the story of their hunts. Others thought they were just decoration. What do you think?

For 15 years, tourists flocked to the caves to view the paintings under modern lighting, but then the caves had to be sealed off to the public. Although the paintings had survived many thousands of years alone in the darkness, they began to horribly deteriorate in just a few years due to exposure to light, as well as to human and air pollution.

ANCIENT EGYPT

In ancient Egypt from about 3,300 B.C. to about 330 B.C., art had the power to transport you from life to death and back again. Ancient Egyptians believed in eternal life after death. For the journey to this new world, a dead body was dried and wrapped in layers of cloth to make a mummy. The mummy was then placed in a decorated coffin. Artists painted portraits on the wooden coffin covers. **Murals**, which are paintings done directly on a wall or ceiling, covered the burial tombs of rich and powerful rulers called pharaohs.

Stand up straight

Egyptian artists were big on rules. All the people they drew were stiff. They often combined a forward-facing body with a face in side-view, or **profile**. Artists used a strict grid-like system—sort of like graph paper—to make sure the bodies were painted in the right **proportion**. With proportion, the sizes of objects make sense in relation to one another, so a leg is larger than a nose, a man is larger than a baby, and a tree is larger than an apple. They also made sure that everything was **symmetrical**, meaning one side was exactly the same as the other.

Way big

The Egyptians liked to carve super-enormous statues. The Great Sphinx of Giza, which is approximately 65 feet (20 meters) high and 260 feet (57 meters) long, is one of the biggest statues ever carved from a single piece of stone.

Picture writing

Ancient Egyptian picture writing is known as **hieroglyphics**, which means "sacred writing." There are more than 1,000 hieroglyphs, or symbols, which can represent an idea or a sound. Hieroglyphics was a total mystery until 1799, when the Rosetta Stone was discovered in Egypt. This stone tablet had text written in hieroglyphics, Greek, and another type of Egyptian writing. The different languages allowed scholars to decode the hieroglyphics.

Can you write your name in hieroglyphics?

GREEK AND ROMAN ART

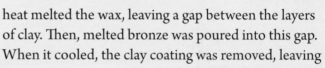

The art of ancient Greece (about 500 B.C.–30 B.C.) and Rome (about 300 B.C.–500 A.D.) is called **Classical Art**. In their art, the Greeks and Romans celebrated the beauty of the human body and the greatness of their gods.

Painting on pottery

Painted pottery was one of the highest forms of art in ancient Greece. The Greeks were skilled at using a potter's wheel. They painted their pottery with scenes of daily life and stories of gods and heroes. Instead of paint, they used **slip**, a mixture of clay and water, to decorate the pottery. The pottery was heated up, or fired, in a very hot oven called a **kiln**.

heat melted the wax, leaving a gap between the layers of clay. Then, melted bronze was poured into this gap. When it cooled, the clay coating was removed, leaving behind the bronze statue.

Greek sculpture

The Greeks were masters at **sculpture**. Traditional sculpture is three-dimensional art that can be viewed from all sides. Most Greek sculpture was of people. Unlike the Egyptians, Greek artists aimed to show humans in a natural way.

The Greeks chiseled marble for their sculpture, and they also used cast bronze. To do this, they first made the sculpture out of clay. Next, they covered the clay with wax and added another layer of clay over it. When the entire piece was fired, the high

Roman sculpture

After the Romans conquered Greece, they modeled their own sculptures after those by Greek artists, who they very much admired. The Romans carved **busts**, or head sculptures, of important people. They gave them realistic faces and features unique to that person. These busts were the first true facial likenesses in art history.

MEDIEVAL ART

For the 1,000 years after the fall of the Roman Empire, in a time called the Middle Ages, or the **Medieval Period**, very little art was produced. Historians named this time the Dark Ages, because it seemed as if the lights had gone out on culture. The **Bayeux Tapestry** was one of the few bright spots.

The Bayeux Tapestry is a picture story **embroidered**, or sewn, with colored wool on a huge piece of linen cloth. It illustrates the Battle of Hastings in 1066 between Normandy and England. The Normans won. The Normans were French, so for the next 300 years, French was spoken in England. An entire workshop of people spent ten years designing and sewing the tapestry. It has more than 70 scenes, each one showing a different event leading up to and including the battle.

Tapestries were hung on the walls of castles during medieval times. The Bayeaux Tapestry is the length of three swimming pools. It is not a woven tapestry but the longest embroidery ever created. It has been kept in Bayeux, France, for as long as anyone knows, and it is one of the most important pieces of art to survive the Middle Ages.

Bayeux Tapestry
(1070S, EMBROIDERY ON LINEN, THE MUSEUM OF BAYEUX TAPESTRY, IN BAYEUX, FRANCE)

ANCIENT ART AROUND THE WORLD

Chinese art

Ancient Chinese emperors spent much of their great wealth on art, paying artists to decorate their palaces with painted scrolls, screens, and fans. When unrolled a little at a time, a scroll tells a story in pictures. **Along the River During the Qingming Festival** is one of the most famous panoramic scrolls and was created by the artist Zhang Zeduan in the early 1100s. The 17-foot-long (5.18 meters) painting shows people, both rich and poor, going about their daily life beside the river and in the marketplace.

The Chinese decorated paper and silk with **calligraphy**, the art of handwriting. *Calligraphy looks like this.*

Chinese potters invented **porcelain**, a thin, strong white ceramic that was shaped into vases and cups. These were then painted with delicate designs in cobalt blue.

Islamic art

Islam is a religion founded by the prophet Mohammad in 622. It spread from Arabia to Asia, Africa, and Europe. Most early Islamic art, such as ceramics, glassware, tile work, carpets, and elaborate carvings, was made to decorate Islamic houses of worship, called **mosques**. Art in mosques is different from Western and Asian art, because it does not show images of humans and living creatures.

The Dome of the Rock in Jerusalem

Along the River During the Qingming Festival

(1100s, ink and color on silk, Palace Museum, in Beijing, China)

17 feet long!

In Islamic art, you often see **patterns** of repeating elements. Most of these patterns are made of geometric shapes, flowers, leaves, or vines. These patterns often take the form of **mosaics**. With mosaic, small pieces of colorful glass, stone, tile, or pottery are arranged in intricate patterns and fixed in plaster or cement. One of the most famous mosaics is in the Dome of the Rock in Jerusalem.

African art

In ancient Africa, **masks** were carved out of wood into the images of ancestors or spirits, most often for use in religious ceremonies. Once a person put on a mask, he or she became the being the mask represented. Masks could be decorated with ivory, precious stones, and animal hair.

Wood statues were also carved in ancient Africa. Statues honored ancestors, kings, and gods. Many have large heads with exaggerated facial features, because Africans believed the head was the most important part of the body.

African wood statue

African mask

Native American totem pole

Native American art

The Native American people on the northwest Pacific coast carved **totem poles** from whole cedar trees. These tall sculptures showed brightly painted animals and people stacked one upon the other. Totem poles were created to record a family history, to tell stories, and for protection.

Basket weaving is one of the oldest Native American crafts. Baskets were woven from roots, bark, grass, and twigs. Different tribes had different styles and used different geometric patterns.

Latin American art

In Central and South America, **gold** was plentiful in the mountains and rivers. Ancient peoples used the dazzling metal to craft jewelry, masks, headpieces, and small statues.

Latin American mask

Limbourg Brothers
late 1380s–1416

and smoke rising from a chimney. When the brothers finished, the duke requested another, longer Book of Hours that he named the ***Très Riches Heures (Very Rich Hours)***. This second book is considered an absolute masterpiece of illumination. There are 206 pages of art and decorative text. Before they could finish the book, all three brothers died the same year in the plague. The bubonic plague, also called the Black Death, was a deadly disease that killed over one-third of the people in Europe in just three years.

Three Dutch brothers named Herman, Paul, and Johan (or Jean) Limbourg turned decorating books into a fine art during the Medieval Period. In the late 1380s, the Limbourg Brothers were born in the Netherlands into an artistic family. Their father was a wood carver and their uncle was an artist who worked for the French queen and the duke of Burgundy. The brothers began painting for the royal family when they were in their teens and were hired by Jean, duc de Berry, the wealthiest art lover in France.

Picture books

The duke asked the Limbourg Brothers to make him a **Book of Hours**, which had prayers for each hour of the day along with a calendar. Most books at that time were religious and were written out entirely by hand by a person called a **scribe**. The duke wanted the Limbourg Brothers to **illuminate** his book with paintings in bright colors decorated with gold. Illuminate means "to fill with light."

The Limbourg Brothers' Book of Hours had the first illustrations with such realistic detail. They were the first to illustrate a scene in the snow, skies with clouds,

Illuminated Letters

In illuminated manuscripts, the first letter on a page is often much larger than the others and filled with decorations. Try making your own!

You Need:
- White paper
- Pencil and eraser
- Black felt-tip marker
- Colored pencils
- Gold crayon

You Create:

1. In the center of the paper, lightly sketch the first initial of your first name. Make it a "bubble letter," leaving room inside to decorate.

2. Inside the letter, draw small pictures that represent you. If you play football, draw a football. If you like music, draw a music note. Or you can just make decorations such as stars, hearts, and smiley faces.

3. Color in your letter and decorations with colored pencils. Use your gold crayon to add bits of gold. Then outline the letter with the black marker.

Construction of the Temple in Jerusalem from the *Très Riches Heures*

(ABOUT 1416, INK AND PAINT ON VELLUM, CONDÉ MUSEUM IN CHANTILLY, FRANCE)

The illustrations in illuminated books are called **miniatures**. They required detailed work with extremely small brushes and a lens to magnify the page. *The Très Riches Heures* disappeared from history for three centuries, and now it is one of the most valuable books in the world.

Books were written by hand until the printing press was used to publish the Gutenburg Bible in 1452. Because very few people knew how to read, very few books were needed.

Both the people and the backgrounds are incredibly detailed.

Illuminated books often took years to finish.

The book is written in Latin, an ancient language.

The art is done on **vellum**, which is made from calfskin.

Jan Van Eyck
1390 *or* 1395-1441

Jan Van Eyck's early life is a mystery. We don't even know the exact year of his birth. All we know is that he was born in Belgium, and his older brother was also a painter. As an adult, he was hired by the duke of Burgundy, Philip the Good, who was the most powerful ruler in the region. Most artists at this time worked on **commission**, meaning they were paid a part of their money up front and the rest when they completed their work, but the duke paid Van Eyck a yearly salary. He really liked how Van Eyck painted!

Know Your Painting Tools

Just as a builder needs a hammer, an artist needs special tools to create.

- A **canvas** is stiff cotton or linen fabric stretched on a frame. Many artists paint on canvas.
- A canvas is often propped up on a wood frame called an **easel** to make it easier for an artist to stand and paint.
- Artists arrange their paint colors on a board called a **palette**. Many palettes are held by putting your thumb through the hole. Artists try to place their colors in the same spots each time. This way, if they want to paint with red, they know exactly where to dip their brush.
- Paint is often placed on a canvas with a **brush.** Brushes are made from stiff or soft hair. Back in Van Eyck's time, all the hair was natural, often coming from sables, squirrels, hogs, and deer. Today many brushes have factory-made hair and come in many different shapes.

Easel
Canvas
Palette

Fan **Filbert** **Angle** **Mop** **Flat**

Brush Types

Detail Guy

Van Eyck is known for all the details in his painting. He was one of the first artists to master the use of **oil paint**, which allowed him to paint this way. **Pigments**, which come from crushed flowers, minerals, or other natural materials, give paint its color. To make oil paint, pigments are mixed with poppy or linseed oil. Unlike other paints, oil paint can be blended right on the canvas. It can be painted in thick layers or thinned with turpentine to be almost transparent, or see-through. Van Eyck used many thin layers. Because oil paint takes a long time to dry, Van Eyck had time to add or change details.

Paint what you see

Van Eyck painted things exactly as he saw them. He made the inside of homes and the texture and shape of everyday objects appear as real as possible. This style is called **Naturalism**.

One burning candle

symbolizes the watchful eye of God.

Mirror — symbolizes that marriage is a contract, or an agreement between people.

Linked hands

symbolize the uniting of two people in marriage.

Puffy dress

Giovanna, in her bright green dress, is not pregnant. Back then, it was very fashionable to hold your dress that way.

Expensive stuff

(clothes, furniture, rug, and chandelier) symbolizes the couple's wealth. The oranges on the windowsill were a luxury in Northern Europe, because this fruit had to be brought in from the south.

Cute dog

symbolizes earthly love and faithfulness. Look how you can see each hair on the dog. Van Eyck used many different colors for the hair.

Van Eyck's personal motto was ALS IXH XAN (As well as I can).

The Arnolfini Portrait

(1434, OIL ON OAK, NATIONAL GALLERY IN LONDON, ENGLAND)

This very detailed oil painting is a double **portrait** of a husband and wife. A portrait is a painting or drawing of a person or people. The man, Giovanni Arnolfini, was a successful Italian banker who lived in the Netherlands in the 1400s. His wife, Giovanna Cenami, came from a wealthy Italian family. This was one of the first portraits to show incredibly lifelike details.

Sandro Botticelli
about 1445–1510

Sandro Botticelli was born in Florence, Italy. His real name was Alessandro Filipepi. His older brother was nicknamed "Botticello," which means "little barrel" in Italian, so people called him "Botticelli." When he was a boy, he became an **apprentice** to a goldsmith. An apprentice is a person who works for a skilled craftsman to learn a trade. He learns by watching and doing, not by going to school. Apprentices were paid very little or nothing at all. The goldsmith taught Botticelli how to paint with fine, delicate lines.

Botticelli switched to painting and had his own studio while he was still in his teens. The Medici family, who ruled Florence, became his **patron**. A patron was a wealthy person, a king, or an important church leader who paid an artist for a work of art. The patron usually got to choose the subject of the painting, the materials used, and when it needed to be finished.

Renaissance artist
Botticelli was an early **Renaissance** artist. Renaissance means "rebirth." The Renaissance took place from about 1350 to 1600, starting in Italy then moving to Northern Europe. During this time, people once again became interested in art and culture. They wanted to fill their houses and churches with remarkable paintings. They became curious about how things worked. Renaissance painters tried to explore the world and understand it.

Ideal beauty
Botticelli was all about beauty. He wanted everyone in his paintings to look beautiful. In the Renaissance, the ideal of beauty was based on Classical examples of Greek and Roman art—elegant noses, high cheekbones, and sculpted jawlines. He used his paintbrush like a pen to make clear outlines around the people he painted.

Egg paint
Botticelli used **tempera paint.** Tempera is made from color pigment mixed with egg yolk. Tempera dates back to the ancient Egyptians. Because it dries fast and hard, tempera works best on smooth surfaces, such as wood panels or poster board. Tempera gives brighter color than oil paint.

Telling the Story . . . Or a Different One

Botticelli is sharing the myth of the Garden of Venus in his painting. Can you help the artist by adding speech bubbles next to each figure? What is Venus saying? Cupid? Zephyrus? Try telling the real myth—or make up a funny one!

La Primavera

(1487-1482, TEMPERA ON PANEL, UFFIZI GALLERY IN FLORENCE, ITALY)

In Italian, *primavera* means "spring." This dreamlike painting shows a scene from a famous myth that takes place in the Garden of Venus. Venus is the Roman goddess of love (Venus is called Aphrodite in Greek mythology). It is always springtime in her garden, and love is always celebrated. *La Primavera* is not a painting of a religious subject, which makes it different from European paintings before the Renaissance.

Botticelli loved to play practical jokes. Once he stuck paper hats on a painting of angels done by his assistants!

Cupid, Venus's mischievous son, flies above with his bow and arrow. He shoots his arrow, burning with the flames of love, to make one of the Three Graces fall in love. He is blindfolded to show that love is blind.

Blue-faced **Zephyrus**, the cold West Wind, falls in love with the nymph Chloris. As he puts her under his spell, the artist shows her turning into Flora, the goddess of flowers.

Mercury, the messenger to the gods, wears his winged boots. His wand pushes the clouds away, so there is always sunshine in Venus's garden.

The three dancing women in white are the **Three Graces**, who give out beauty throughout the world.

Venus, the goddess of love and the symbol of spring, is in the center. The dark leaves around her make her stand out. She has a motherly look to her.

Leonardo da Vinci
1452-1519

Leonardo carried the Mona Lisa with him everywhere he traveled.

Leonardo da Vinci did practically everything, and he did it all amazingly well! He was a painter, sculptor, architect, engineer, inventor, and musician. Because of his many talents, he's called the ultimate "Renaissance Man." Born in the town of Vinci, Italy, he was given the last name da Vinci, which means "from Vinci." Back then, people often took the name of their towns.

Leonardo loved to draw. He apprenticed with a famous painter and sculptor in Florence. He would mix colors, clean brushes, and ready the walls or wood for painting. Young Leonardo was so talented that one day he painted a very realistic-looking angel. His teacher threw down his paintbrush in jealousy, declaring he would never paint again (he was lying!). Royalty, wealthy patrons, and even the pope asked Leonardo to paint for them. He took on a lot of work, but he was easily distracted. He often didn't finish what he promised.

Curious about it all

Leonardo had a never-ending thirst for knowledge. He studied nature carefully. He was fascinated by the inner workings of machines. At night he would secretly dissect, or cut apart, dead bodies that he got from hospitals or prisons to learn human **anatomy**. Anatomy is how the body and its organs fit together. He used all this knowledge to make his paintings look more realistic.

Secret notebooks

Leonardo filled many notebooks with nearly 2,500 sketches, diagrams, and notes. A **sketch** is a quick drawing. Everything he discovered and every new idea he had went into his notebooks. He wrote all his notes backward in "mirror writing," so others could not read his secrets. The only way to decipher his notebooks was to hold them up to a mirror.

This is what mirror writing looks like! Now you try it.

A Look at His Inventions

Leonardo was one of the greatest inventors and scientists in history. His ideas were years, even centuries, ahead of their time. Here are some things he came up with and sketched in his notebooks:

- Armored tank
- Water-operated alarm clock (he had trouble getting up in the mornings)
- Bicycle
- Car
- Parachute
- Submarine
- Hang glider
- Helicopter

Da Vinci Tank **Modern Tank**

Da Vinci Helicopter **Modern Helicopter**

People feel that her eyes follow you no matter where you stand.

Mona Lisa

(1503–1506, OIL ON WOOD, LOUVRE MUSEUM IN PARIS, FRANCE)

The *Mona Lisa* is the most famous painting in the world, and her smile is the most famous smile. Who was she? Her full name was Madonna Lisa di Antonio Maria Gherardini. She was the wife of a wealthy man from Florence who hired Leonardo to paint her portrait. It took Leonardo about four years to finish the picture, which is actually very small in size.

This painting is so famous that it was stolen right off the wall of the Louvre in 1911. After a lot of detective work, the *Mona Lisa* was discovered in Italy two years later, and the art thief was arrested.

Leonardo did not outline his people. His study of nature made him realize that people and animals don't have outlines. He used a technique called **sfumato**, which comes from the Latin word that means "smoky." With *sfumato*, there are no harsh outlines, and one color is blended into another in a soft, hazy way. Look how the background landscape seems to disappear into the mist. Also see how her lips blend into her skin.

What does her mysterious smile mean? Is she keeping a secret? Is she happy? Or is she sad? What do you think?

The painting got its name because "Mona" is short for "Madonna," which means "my lady" in Italian.

She had to sit completely still for many hours, day after day. Leonardo brought in clowns and musicians to entertain her.

Leonardo gave Mona Lisa a natural pose. Her hands are especially relaxed.

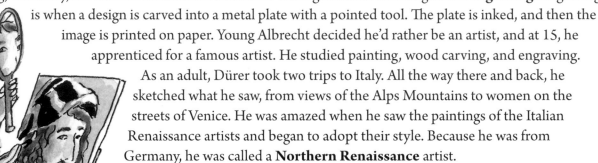

Albrecht Dürer
1471-1528

Albrecht Dürer was fascinated by nature as a young child, and he loved to sketch animals and plants. He was born in Nuremberg, Germany, the third of 18 children. His father was a goldsmith and taught him **engraving**. Engraving is when a design is carved into a metal plate with a pointed tool. The plate is inked, and then the image is printed on paper. Young Albrecht decided he'd rather be an artist, and at 15, he apprenticed for a famous artist. He studied painting, wood carving, and engraving.

As an adult, Dürer took two trips to Italy. All the way there and back, he sketched what he saw, from views of the Alps Mountains to women on the streets of Venice. He was amazed when he saw the paintings of the Italian Renaissance artists and began to adopt their style. Because he was from Germany, he was called a **Northern Renaissance** artist.

Look, it's me!
At age 13, Dürer was one of the first artists known to draw a **self-portrait**. A self-portrait is a drawing or painting an artist makes of himself or herself by looking at his or her reflection in a mirror. He painted many self-portraits at different ages throughout his life, the same way you get class pictures taken every year.

Just add water
Dürer was one of the first artists to paint with **watercolor**. In watercolor, pigment is mixed with water. The paint is thin and the color is **translucent**, which means the paper or canvas shows through.

Painting with Watercolors

Some artists love watercolors because they think drips or streaks can look beautiful. Other artists hate them because once you put the paint on the paper, there's no fixing it. Watercolor is applied in thin, watery layers called **washes**. The amount of water you use changes how dark or light the color appears. With watercolor, you can blend colors and soften the lines between them, so one color fades into the other. Many watercolor artists leave areas of their white paper untouched, so the paper's whiteness, and not the paint, creates sparkles of sunlight.

A Young Hare

(1502, WATERCOLOR AND GOUACHE ON PAPER,
ALBERTINA MUSEUM IN VIENNA, AUSTRIA)

Dürer was one of the first artists to paint an animal all on its own. This painting of a hare, an animal similar to a rabbit except with longer ears and legs, is extremely detailed and looks almost like a scientific illustration or a photograph. Painting this hare took a lot of patience. The light strikes the hare on the left side and highlights the ears and the fur along that side. Its eyes sparkle with life. *A Young Hare* remains one of the most famous animal portraits in the world.

Dürer built up the fur using brushstrokes of light and dark brown watercolor. The fur points in many different directions.

The white highlights were done in **gouache**, a thicker watercolor that's not seethrough.

Some people say he captured a hare in the wild and kept it in a cage in his workshop, so he could use it as a model. Others say he used a stuffed hare. What do you think?

Even though the title is *A Young Hare*, it's actually a full grown hare.

Dürer signed and dated his drawings and paintings with a logo he designed himself.

If people knew how hard I worked . . . it wouldn't seem so wonderful at all.

Michelangelo
1475-1564

Few people are famous enough to be called only by their first names. Michelangelo is one of them. Born in Florence, Italy, Michelangelo's full name is Michelangelo di Lodovico Buonarroti Simoni. His mother was ill when he was young, and a family of stonecutters took care of him. Growing up during the Renaissance, Michelangelo knew he wanted to be an artist. He apprenticed to both a painter and a sculptor and then moved to Rome. He was a devout Christian, and most of his art was religious.

Taking credit

He made his first great sculpture before he was even 25 years old. It's called the *Pietà* and shows Jesus Christ lying dead in his mother Mary's lap. Michelangelo carved it from one block of marble using chisels, hammers, and pumice stones. Before Michelangelo, sculpture had been very stiff and without emotion, but here, you can see and feel Mary's sadness.

The *Pietà* is the only piece of work Michelangelo ever signed. The story goes that, as he was delivering the sculpture himself, he overheard spectators saying that he was too young to have really created the work. Michelangelo was angry, and that night he returned and chiseled his name on it.

Trapped!

David was Michelangelo's next important sculpture. It is 17 feet tall (5.18 meters) and carved out of a huge block of marble. It shows the biblical hero David bravely holding his slingshot before his battle with Goliath. Michelangelo once said that the sculpture was trapped inside the block of marble, and it was his job to let it out.

Upside-Down Art

Experience how Michelangelo felt while painting the Sistine Chapel ceiling!

You Need:
- Large sheet of white paper
- Masking tape
- Watercolor paints
- Paint brush
- Water
- A low table

You Create:

1. Have someone help you tape your paper to the underside of a table. Now lie on your back under the table, looking up at your paper. You can put a pillow under your head.

2. Wet your brush and have an assistant hold your tray of watercolors next to you. Paint whatever you want. How does your arm feel? Is it tired? Michelangelo painted like this for four years!

The Sistine Chapel
(1508–1512, FRESCO, THE VATICAN PALACE IN ITALY)

In addition to making sculptures, Michelangelo trained as a painter in both oil and **fresco**. Fresco is a technique of painting directly on a wall or ceiling. Colored pigment powder is added to wet plaster, and the color becomes permanent when the plaster dries. Painters have to work very quickly.

In 1508, Pope Julius II ordered Michelangelo to fresco the huge ceiling of the Sistine Chapel in the Vatican Palace with scenes from the Old Testament. Michelangelo didn't want to do it. He liked making sculptures more than painting, but since it was the pope who asked, he had no choice but to agree. Early on, Michelangelo became annoyed by his assistants and sent most of them away. He worked for four years on his ceiling masterpiece, painting more than 300 figures. No two of the 300 people look alike.

Michelangelo painted nine Old Testament stories in rectangular panels that run the length of the vaulted ceiling. He placed the story of Adam and Eve at its center, with the famous image of God stretching out his hand to give Adam life.

The enormous ceiling is 66 feet (20 meters) above the ground. He worked high above the floor, lying on his back on scaffolding, which are raised wood platforms.

He used a style called **trompe l'oeil**, which is French for "fool the eye." This technique makes things look so real that the artist fools the viewer.

He also painted seven Prophets and five Sibyls along the edges of the ceiling, as well as Christ's ancestors in the triangular-shaped sections.

Pieter Bruegel
about 1525-1569

Pieter Bruegel is another painter whose life is a bit of a mystery. He was born in the Netherlands. He apprenticed for a painter and publisher in Antwerp, which was a city of wealthy bankers who hoped to fill their homes with art. He took a trip to Italy, and on the way back home, he became fascinated by the Alps Mountains and surrounding forests.

Soon, Bruegel began painting **landscapes**. A landscape shows the land around you. Renaissance painters painted portraits of people in a realistic, natural setting. Bruegel felt the landscape alone could be the focus of a painting.

The fake peasant

Bruegel liked to paint peasants, or farmers, in the countryside, but he wasn't a peasant himself. In fact, he was quite wealthy and lived in a large city. In order to paint them, Bruegel, along with one of his patrons from the city, would dress in peasant clothing and go out to the countryside. Together they would sneak into fairs and weddings, pretending they were invited guests. He was so good at his disguises that his friends called him "Peasant Bruegel." Bruegel studied the rural people's looks and gestures and then made quick sketches. Later, he would go back to his city studio and paint the scenes he remembered.

His secret

Bruegel had a secret to his art. He drew everything he saw—and from every direction. So if he saw a chicken, he'd sketch it from the front, the back, and each side. He'd even sketch it from above! When he was in his studio, he'd lay out all his sketches and be able to paint the object from whichever direction worked best.

Fitting It Together

Let's say you decide to draw a landscape picture of your school playground during recess. Where will you put the people? The playground equipment? The fence? Every artist must decide how the colors, shapes, and forms fit together on his or her paper or canvas. This is called **composition**. If you want your painting to look realistic, you need to draw in **proportion**. This means you'd draw a squirrel much smaller than a person— unless, of course, it's a mutant monster squirrel!

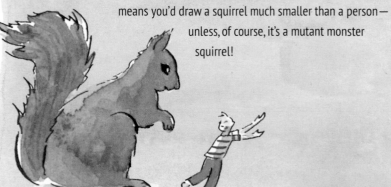

The Harvesters

(1565, OIL ON WOOD, THE METROPOLITAN MUSEUM OF ART IN NEW YORK, NEW YORK)

The Harvesters is part of a **series** of paintings showing the different seasons of the year. A series is many pictures about the same subject. Bruegel's series, which we think had six paintings in total, was called *The Months of the Year*. Each detailed painting celebrates a different season. Can you guess what season and months *The Harvesters* pictures?

Men and women are hard at work harvesting the golden wheat. This is shown by their movements, not by the expressions on their faces.

Bruegel painted the scene from a bird's-eye view, as if he were looking down at it from above.

The group of peasants resting and eating their midday meal at the bottom right balances the view of the village at the top left. The diagonal swoosh of the grain divides the two, making the picture **balanced** and pleasing to view.

You can feel the heat of summer through the use of hot yellow and bright green paint.

He is known as Pieter Bruegel the Elder because his son, who is also named Pieter, was a well-known artist, too.

Bruegel was interested in how different the land looked from one month to the next. He thought the change of seasons told the story of the people and their lives. How does your street and the people on it change in summer, fall, winter, and spring?

Diego Velázquez
1599–1660

A painter of royalty, Diego Velázquez was born in Seville, Spain. At age 12, he was apprenticed to the best painter in the city. Early on, he showed he could paint people incredibly well. Religious paintings were in style then, but Velázquez wanted to paint portraits. He set up his own shop and by age 21 had an apprentice of his own.

One day, he was invited to Madrid to do a portrait of the newly crowned king, Philip IV. The young king was thrilled with his portrait. He declared that Velázquez would be the only court painter allowed to paint his portrait. The king and Velázquez became good friends, which was unusual. The king even had a special chair placed in the artist's studio, so he could sit and watch his friend paint.

Spanish art

The 1600s were called the "Golden Age" of Spanish painting. Spanish artists were influenced by Italian art. At this time, Spain was a leader in exploration to the New World and the Far East and had become a very wealthy country. The people of Spain began to spend their new wealth on art.

Baroque painter

Velázquez painted in a style called **Baroque**, which refers to the period between 1600 and 1750. A Baroque painting is very elaborate with a lot of detail and rich colors. Velázquez used this dramatic style to make the people in his picture look beautiful and grand.

Say Cheese!

It's an important day, such as your birthday, and your whole family has gathered together. You want to remember this special day, so what do you do? You probably pull out a camera and snap a photo. That works today, but **photography** was only invented in the mid-1800s. Before that time, you had to hire an artist to have your portrait painted.

Las Meniñas

(ABOUT 1656, OIL ON CANVAS, PRADO MUSEUM IN MADRID, SPAIN)

This large painting makes us think. The title means "The Maids of Honor." The king's five-year-old daughter, Princess Margarita, is in the center. Her maids of honor surround her. But is this really a portrait of a young girl? Why are only her maids looking at her and everyone else is staring into the distance? Take a closer look—the scene is *a lot* more complicated!

This is a painting about painting portraits. First we have the princess and her maids. Now look to the left. That's a self-portrait of Velázquez, the artist, painting on a large canvas. Wait! Who is he painting, since he is standing *behind* the little girl? Look at the mirror at the back of the room. Reflected in it are the king and queen. Are they the subjects posing for the artist's portrait? The princess seems to be looking at the king and queen, too.

Velázquez has the red cross of the Knights of the Order of Santiago on his shirt. Only the king could make someone a knight. When this painting was finished, Velázquez hadn't gotten the honor yet, so he had to take the painting back and put it in.

In the background, we can see a nun and a priest talking. They might symbolize how important the Church was to royal life.

If a kings and queens couldn't go to an event, they would send their portraits instead!

The people on the right side are the court jesters, who provided entertainment for royal families. Dwarves were often employed as court jesters. One jester playfully steps on the big sleepy dog.

The king and queen must be standing where we the viewers are standing. This makes us feel as if we are part of the group.

Rembrandt Van Rijn
1606-1669

Rembrandt is another one-name painter, and he is famous for his dramatic use of **light and shadow**. The son of a wealthy miller in the Netherlands, Rembrandt decided to leave school when he was 15 to study art as an apprentice. He started his own studio at age 19. For the next 20 years, he was the go-to portrait painter for the richest families in Amsterdam. He was one of the first painters not only to work for patrons but to sell his works to "regular" people, too.

Copycat

Rembrandt had a very successful workshop with almost 50 young assistants working for him and copying his style. He often signed their paintings as his own. Some art historians have had trouble telling which paintings were fully painted by him.

There's a monkey in my art!

Rembrandt suffered many personal tragedies. His wife died after only eight years of marriage, and three of his children died while still babies. In grief, he spent more money than he had. He was very stubborn, and as his fortune turned, his stubbornness increased. One time, he refused to remove a monkey he'd painted in a family portrait. The family argued that they didn't even own a monkey. Rembrandt insisted that the monkey stay in. The family wouldn't take the painting and wouldn't pay him. He decided he'd rather starve than change his painting.

Light and dark

When an artist paints an object in light colors and surrounds it with dark colors, it's called **contrast**. Contrast makes the object stand out, or "pop." For added drama, Rembrandt often placed an extremely light area right next to a very shaded dark area. This bold light/dark effect is called **chiaroscuro**.

The faces show the excitement at the scientific discovery. They are bright compared with the dark background. The light/dark contrast makes us feel the tension in the operating room, and it draws our eyes to the chief surgeon's face, not to his hands.

The Anatomy Lesson of Dr. Tulp

(1632, OIL ON CANVAS, MAURITSHUIS ROYAL PICTURE GALLERY IN THE HAGUE, THE NETHERLANDS)

Rembrandt was known for his lively **group portraits**. Here, Dr. Tulp dissects a body while seven other doctors watch. Back then, people paid to watch dissections in an operating theater, much in the same way we go out to the movies today. Dissections were done only in the winter when the theater stayed ice-cold, so the body would not decay quickly. With this painting, Rembrandt hoped to capture the drama of the event.

Rembrandt turned each man's head in a different direction to make the composition more interesting. He also arranged the men in a pyramid shape.

The dead man is a criminal known as "The Kid."

Rembrandt added pink to Dr. Tulp's skin to contrast him with the pale corpse.

In the Shadows

If an artist wants to focus only on the shape of a person, he or she will paint a **silhouette**. A silhouette is a dark figure in front of a light background, as if the person were standing in front of a light. You can make your own silhouette.

You Need:
- Large white drawing paper
- Black construction paper
- Tape
- Glue stick
- Scissors
- Pencil
- Lamp
- Chair

You Create:

1. Tape the white paper to a wall. Set up the chair alongside the paper. The paper should be at the same height as the chair. Make the room completely dark and shine the lamp on the chair.

2. Have a friend or family member sit in the chair facing sideways. His or her **profile** should appear in shadow on the white paper. Adjust the lamp to get the clearest shadow.

3. Using a pencil, carefully trace the outline of the person's head, neck, and shoulders onto the white paper. Make sure the person sits very still.

4. Take the white paper off the wall. Lightly glue the white paper to the black paper, outline side up.

5. Cut along the outline carefully. Peel off the white paper and glue the black silhouette to a fresh piece of white or colored paper.

Jan Vermeer
1632-1675

Very little is known about Dutch artist Jan Vermeer. There are only 35 recognized works by Vermeer. He was born in Delft, in the Netherlands. His father was a silk weaver, art dealer, and tavern owner. When he was 20, his father died and Vermeer took over the inn and the art dealership. It is not known whether Vermeer learned how to paint as an apprentice or on his own.

Home, sweet home

In the early 1600s, the Netherlands was making a lot of money from the Spice Islands they'd taken over in Indonesia. Wealthy Dutch families wanted to own paintings that showed their daily life and the landscape around them. Vermeer painted exactly this type of painting. He is famous for his scenes set inside the home. All his works have a sense of quiet and stillness.

Color combo

Vermeer is famous for how he handled color. One of his favorite combinations was yellow, blue, and gray. Do you have a favorite color combo?

Faker!

A **forger** is someone who copies an artist's style and falsely signs the artist's name to a painting. Then he sells that painting for a lot of money, pretending it is an original. In the 1930s, a Dutch artist named Han Van Meegeren forged a number of Vermeers and sold them for millions of dollars. Many important art historians were tricked and thought the paintings were true Vermeers. Van Meegeren had created a technique to make the paint look old. He was arrested in 1945 and spent one year in jail.

Vermeer was called a "Little Master" because he produced paintings that were small enough to hang in a home.

The Girl with a Pearl Earring

(ABOUT 1665, OIL ON CANVAS, MAURITSHUIS ROYAL PICTURE GALLERY
IN THE HAGUE, THE NETHERLANDS)

This portrait is sometimes called the "Dutch Mona Lisa." No one knows who this girl is. She appears to be a commoner, yet her pearl earring is enormous and expensive. With her wide eyes gazing directly at us as she glances over her shoulder, she seems about to tell us something.

The black background makes the girl pop out at us. The background was originally a grayish green, but it blackened over time.

Vermeer painted several thin layers of paint on top of one another, letting the bottom layers glow through. He blended his brushstrokes until they were almost invisible.

The shade of bright blue on her silk turban is called "Vermeer Blue." Vermeer mixed his colors from his own recipes, and his pigments were very intense. Making this ultramarine blue was very expensive. He had to crush a semiprecious stone from Afghanistan called lapis lazuli.

The turban she wears is exotic for the Netherlands. Artists at this time liked to paint turbans because the folds and rich fabric showed off their painting skills.

Let's Talk Color

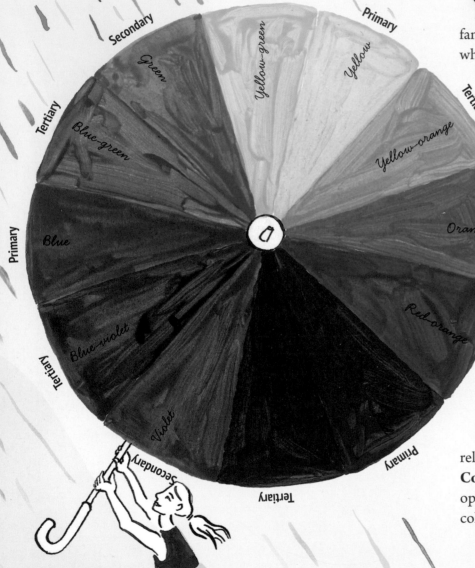

Tertiary · Primary · Yellow · Tertiary · Secondary · Tertiary · Primary · Tertiary · Primary · Secondary · Primary

Yellow-green · Green · Blue-green · Blue · Blue-violet · Violet · Orange · Yellow-orange · Red-orange

Primary colors

You stand in front of a blank piece of paper, just as a famous artist stands before his or her canvas. You know what you want to paint. But what colors should you use? This is a very important choice. Color gives a painting a mood. Color changes how we view different objects and scenes.

Color Recipes

Red, blue, and yellow are the **three primary** colors. Primary colors cannot be created from other colors. They can be mixed to make all the other colors of the rainbow.

Secondary colors are the three colors you get when you mix one primary color with another primary color.

Tertiary Colors, or the third group of colors, are the six colors formed by mixing one primary and one secondary color.

Spin the Color Wheel

A **color wheel** shows the relationship between colors. **Complementary colors** are opposite one another on the color wheel.

Red and Green
Blue and Orange
Yellow and Purple

What happens if you mix complementary colors together? You get brown.

Analogous colors are colors side-by-side on the color wheel, such as blue-green and blue.

Tints are colors with white added to make them lighter. Add white to purple and you get lavender. Add white to red and you get pink.

Shades are colors mixed with black. Black makes a color darker. Add black to green, and you get forest green. Add black to blue and you get navy.

Monochromatic colors are all the colors from one family, just with white or black added. For example, pink, red, and burgundy are monochromatic.

Warm colors

Color Temperature

Red, yellow, and orange are called **warm colors**. These sunny colors give a painting a feeling of warmth. Warm colors make objects appear closer in a picture.

Colors with blue added to them are called **cool colors.** Blue, green, and purple are cool colors. Cool colors make objects appear farther away in a picture.

Complementary colors

Tints

Shades

Monochromatic colors

Cool colors

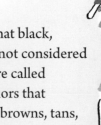

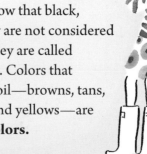

Earth colors

Did you know that black, white, and gray are not considered true colors? They are called **neutral colors.** Colors that resemble the soil—browns, tans, warms grays, and yellows—are called **earth colors.**

Francisco de Goya
1746-1828

Francisco de Goya was born in a small town in northern Spain. His father was a **gilder** and taught his son how to paint. A gilder applies thin layers of gold to paintings, statues, furniture, and church altarpieces. At age 14, Goya became an apprentice to a well-known painter. Goya didn't like to follow rules, so they didn't get along. He moved to Madrid and married the sister of the court painter to the king of Spain. He then became his assistant. Goya moved up and eventually became the main court painter to three generations of kings.

Next, please

For a time, Goya was known as Spain's top portrait painter. The members of the royal family wanted their portraits painted by Goya. He was inspired by the realism of Velázquez's art, which still hung on the palace walls.

Romanticism

Goya was a **Romantic** artist. Romantic art highlighted feelings and showed strong emotions. Goya used softer brushstrokes.

When the world got quiet . . .

At age 46, Goya suffered a terrible illness. As a result, he became deaf. No longer able to hear, Goya was always in a bad mood. His paintings turned darker in color and subject. He used a lot of black paint, and he drew monsters and skeletons. The portraits he painted for the king became dark and stiff. Naturally, the king wasn't pleased and stopped having Goya paint for him.

In Black and White

Painting with the neutral colors black, white, and gray creates a serious mood. Try a picture using only these colors. Paint a scene, such as a forest, your backyard, or your street. When the paint is dry, you can add one dash of color for **emphasis**, such as a red bird, a yellow flower, or an orange bicycle.

When Goya lost his hearing, he heard a high-pitched buzzing in his ears for the rest of his life. Now you can understand why he was so cranky!

The Third of May, 1808

(1814, OIL ON CANVAS, PRADO MUSEUM IN MADRID, SPAIN)

The army of Napoleon, the ruler of France, brutally occupied Goya's country of Spain. On May 2, 1808, the people of Spain rose up and rebelled with only knives and sticks. The next night, Napoleon's soldiers rounded up these rebels and many innocent bystanders. They paraded them before a firing squad and shot them. Six years later, after the Spanish king was back in power, Goya recorded the raw horror of that night. In the past, paintings of war had mostly celebrated victories. Goya wanted to show the senseless violence of war. In this painting, he made the victims the heroes. When asked why he painted this picture, Goya said, "To warn men never to do it again."

The composition is one of diagonals—the line of the hill, the line of the firing squad, and the man's V-shaped arms.

A dark sky looms over the scene, adding to the grim mood.

The men pray and weep. You can see the fear in their faces.

Goya didn't show the faces of the men in the firing squad. In their military uniforms, they are faceless evil.

The bodies of the men who have already been shot lie on the ground. Goya wanted people to see how bloody these killings were. One dead man's arms are in the same position as the man in white's arms.

The light comes from a huge lantern, as if a spotlight is thrown on a secret scene.

The man at the center is a symbol of all the other victims. He is dressed in pure white and yellow and has his arms raised in surrender. You can see the fear and helplessness in his wide eyes. His bright clothing stands out from the dark background.

Katsushika Hokusai
1760–1849

Woodblock Print Card

You Need:

- Styrofoam meat tray (ask butcher for clean ones) or a Styrofoam plate
- Acrylic paint (any color)
- Foam brush
- Ballpoint pen
- Scissors
- 8 ½ x 11 white paper, folded in half to make a card

You Create:

1. Cut your Styrofoam into a square or rectangle.

2. Use the tip of a ballpoint pen to etch a picture or a design with swirls, dots, and lines into the Styrofoam. Remember, your picture will print as a mirror image.

3. Using your foam brush, gently cover the entire square of Styrofoam with a layer of paint. Do not press the paint into the indents your pen made—you want these areas to print white.

4. Flip the Styrofoam over and press it firmly to the outside of your folded white paper. Quickly pull it up and see your print. You may have to try a few times to get the amount of paint just right.

Katsushika Hokusai was one of the most important early Japanese artists. He was especially famous for his landscapes. Born in Edo, Japan (now called Tokyo), he started as an apprentice to a printmaker. The printmaker threw him out of his workshop because, instead of doing exactly what the man said, Hokusai liked to experiment and try new techniques.

Woodblock prints

Hokusai was most famous for his **woodblock prints**. He would draw a picture on very thin paper and then trace the drawing on a block of wood. Then, he carved away the wood around the lines so that the picture he had drawn was raised from the surface of the block. Next, he coated the raised areas with ink, and a piece of paper was pressed on top. The print came out as a mirror image.

A different block was used for each color. Sometimes as many as 12 blocks were used for one picture. Hokusai's prints were so popular, the blocks used to make them wore out. In his lifetime, he completed over 30,000 works of art.

Celebrate nature

Hokusai was a master of **ukiyo-e**, which in Japanese means "pictures of the floating world." Ukiyo-e painters hoped to celebrate the fragile beauty of the natural world.

Hokusai never cleaned his studio. When the place became too dirty to work, he'd move instead of clean up!

The stamp of Japanese characters in the corner is how Hokusai signed his work.

Snow-capped Mount Fuji is framed by the foamy curve of the wave.

In this dangerous moment, the artist captures the movement of the claw-like wave overpowering the helpless boats.

A smaller wave has the same shape as Mount Fuji.

Hokusai used sea-blue inks on white paper.

The Great Wave off Kanagawa

(1830–1832, INK AND COLOR ON PAPER, THE METROPOLITAN MUSEUM OF ART IN NEW YORK, NEW YORK, THE ART INSTITUTE OF CHICAGO IN ILLINOIS, AND THE BRITISH MUSEUM IN LONDON, ENGLAND)

This print is one in a series entitled *Thirty-six Views of Mount Fuji.* Mount Fuji is the highest mountain in Japan. It is the sacred symbol of Japan and its name has many different meanings, including "eternal life." In this print, a towering wave is about to crash onto three tiny boats filled with fishermen. The waves roar, but the mountain is silent and unmoving. Hokusai shows us the power of nature.

My name is . . .

Back in Hokusai's day, it was not unusual in Japan to change one's name, sometimes more than once. Hokusai changed his name more than 30 times! Hokusai, the name he kept the longest, means "Star of the Northern Constellation."

Show time

Hokusai liked an audience. He'd do public performances where he would paint hanging upside down or with the brush between his toes or in his mouth. Once, he painted two sparrows on one small grain of rice. Another time, he made a painting so enormous, people had to stand on their roofs to see it!

Édouard Manet
1832-1883

Édouard Manet was one of the most important painters of the 1800s. He was born in Paris, France, into a wealthy and well-educated family. His father wanted him to become a lawyer, but Manet refused. So his father made him join the navy. Manet was a horrible sailor and spent most of his time on the ship drawing pictures of his fellow shipmates. When he came back after a year at sea, he begged his father to let him be an artist. He studied for six years with a famous painter in Paris and also traveled to Italy, Germany, and the Netherlands to see great paintings. He spent his days in museums, copying the paintings of the Old Masters over and over, which was a popular teaching method at that time.

Keeping it real

He returned to Paris and made **Realism** the focus of his art. In the 1800s, the world was becoming more industrialized. Cities grew. Artists wanted to paint scenes of ordinary life. Manet often took his models from the streets, painting them in their everyday clothing, doing the things they normally did.

People were shocked by the realism in his paintings. They thought his colors were too harsh and that some of his models were ugly. Manet tried to exhibit his works with the Parisian masters, but they rejected him and criticized his modern way of painting.

Great too late

Manet was upset that no one appreciated his art, but he kept on painting. He is now credited with helping make way for a new style of painting, called Impressionism,

by bridging the ways of the past with those of the modern day. (We'll learn more about Impressionism later.) Toward the end of his life, he was included in exhibitions and people finally realized his talent. At his funeral, artist Edgar Degas said of Manet: "He was greater than we thought."

There's a story that, when Manet was in the navy, the boat's captain knew he was a good artist and had him "touch up" the food so it wouldn't look so rotten and spoiled.

The Fifer

(1866, OIL ON CANVAS, ORSAY MUSEUM IN PARIS, FRANCE)

Manet painted this portrait after seeing portraits by Velázquez hanging in the Prado Museum on a visit to Spain. Plucking a nameless fife player from a military band, Manet painted this normal little boy as if he were royalty. He used bold brushstrokes and flat areas of color. This honest and straightforward image is one of the first works of modern art.

A fife is a flute-like instrument.

What's in the background? Nothing—and at that time, this was very shocking.

Because there's no background, the vivid red and solid black of the boy's uniform jump out.

This painting was criticized for being too simple and was rejected for Paris exhibitions.

There are no shadows, which gives the painting the same flatness found in photographs.

Paint with Five Senses

Artists use all five senses—sight, sound, taste, touch, and smell—to tell a story or show emotions. Why don't you try it, too?

TASTE: Sit at a table with a piece of paper and a pencil. Tie a blindfold over your eyes. Have someone place a plate of different foods in front of you (try a slice of lemon, a cookie, or a piece of cheese). As you bite into each food, try to draw what you taste.

SMELL: Now do the same thing, but this time, bring the food up to your nose and inhale. Draw what you smell.

TOUCH: Set up the same way again, but this time, touch the foods. Draw what you feel.

SIGHT: Take off the blindfold, and draw what you see on the plate in front of you.

SOUND: Keep your blindfold on. Listen to the sounds around you and draw what you hear.

Winslow Homer
1836-1910

Winslow Homer painted the world as he witnessed it, from the horror of war to the beauty and power of the ocean. He was born in Boston, Massachusetts, and his father sold hardware. His mother was a talented artist who painted watercolors of flowers, birds, and butterflies. She was his first art teacher. Homer's first job was as a printmaker in Boston. He hated having to answer to a boss and promised himself that, from then on, he would always be his own boss.

Homer moved to New York City to make illustrations for the largest magazine in the city, called *Harper's Weekly*. Not long after he moved, the Civil War began, and the magazine sent him to Virginia to sketch what he saw on the battlefields. His art back then was what you see photojournalists do today. Homer's drawings were more thoughtful than bloody, showing the soldiers in their camps or as prisoners of war. Through his Civil War art, Homer became famous.

At home in nature

Homer was a **Realist** painter. He always wanted to show the true relationship between people and nature in his art. As a boy, Homer had enjoyed playing in the outdoors, and now he enjoyed painting the outdoors. He moved to Maine and fell in love with the sea.

He is best known for his **seascapes**. A seascape is a painting in which the sea is the most important subject. With bold, quick brushstrokes, Homer painted the power of the sea—the crash of the waves, the spray of the saltwater, and the force of the wind.

Ready to paint

At age 37, Homer began to use watercolors. Painting with watercolor requires an artist to work faster than with oil paint, and it takes a certain skill that Homer mastered. He carried his watercolors with him everywhere, so he could quickly set up and paint whenever he spotted a great scene.

Homer liked to be by himself, and his studio in Maine was on a remote cliff overlooking the ocean.

Breezing Up (A Fair Wind)

(1873–76, OIL ON CANVAS, NATIONAL GALLERY OF ART IN WASHINGTON, D.C.)

This famous painting shows a father and his three sons out at sea in a small sailboat. The wind fills the sail on this breezy summer day. Homer lets us feel the motion of the boat, as if we are sitting in it, too. The waves are choppy, but the sailors are relaxed. The painting is uplifting and sends a message of hope. *A Fair Wind* was Homer's original title, but it was changed to *Breezing Up* at one of his first art shows.

Homer used a lot of triangles in this painting. How many can you find?

A **focal point** is the first thing that stands out in a painting. What do you think the focal point is here?

The boy holding the rudder and steering the boat looks toward the horizon. This may symbolize his looking forward to the future.

Homer painted with soft, warm colors. The sunlight on the water makes it appear as if the sea is made up of different colors.

As Blue as the Ocean

What color is the water in an ocean or lake? Did you say blue? What does that mean? There are many shades of blue: aqua, turquoise, sky blue, steel blue, cornflower blue, royal blue, navy, and indigo.

Using only blue, white, and black paint, mix as many shades/tones as you can. For every new blue you mix, paint a small square on a piece of white paper and give the color your own descriptive name. How about dolphin blue or dragonfly blue?

We were introducing you to artists in order of their birth dates and then along came Monet! Because he started Impressionism, we thought you'd want to hear about him before the others.

Claude Monet
1840-1926

Forget what you see before your eyes, a tree, a house, a field, and simply think: here's a small blue square, there's a pink rectangle, there's a yellow streak, and paint what appears before you.

Claude Monet was the first Impressionist. The son of a grocer from Le Havre, France, Monet never liked school. He felt trapped in the classroom and longed to be outside. When he was old enough, he moved to Paris to paint.

At the time, the kind of paintings being shown in Paris had a lot of dark colors and told serious stories about history, religion, and mythology. Monet found them depressing. He preferred bright colors and subjects drawn from everyday life. But no one liked Monet's loose, sketchy style and bright dabs of paint. They thought his pictures looked as if they weren't finished. Monet didn't care. He didn't sell anything, but he kept painting in his own unique way.

What is Impressionism?

The term **Impressionism** comes from one of Monet's paintings, *Impression: Sunrise*. The painting shows two small boats and the rising sun. Monet was not interested in showing the exact likeness of an object or a scene but rather his impression of it. Critics labeled this loose style of art "impressionism" to mock it, but Monet and his artist friends liked the term. The Impressionists exhibited together as a group and explored the way light fell on shapes and colors.

Monet believed that the color black did not exist in nature.

All in a row

Monet did several **theme paintings**, which is a series all on the same subject. He completed more than 30 paintings of the Cathedral at Rouen and about as many of the haystacks in a field near his house. He painted them on different days, at different times, and in different weather to show how their appearance changed depending on the light. He'd bring wheelbarrows filled with all his canvases and work on the whole series, moving from canvas to canvas as the light moved. He'd paint each canvas at exactly the same time every day. Monet wanted to prove that everything around us is constantly changing.

Let's go outside

Before 1840, artists sketched outdoors but had to return to the studio to paint. Then, manufacturers discovered how to put oil paint in small tubes. The Impressionists found that they could capture the beauty of nature if they painted the entire painting outside, or "**en plein air**" in French. Artists had to work fast because the light changed rapidly. With little time for mixing paint, Monet used quick dabs of pure color.

Japanese Footbridge and the Water Lily Pool

(1899, OIL ON CANVAS, PHILADELPHIA MUSEUM OF ART IN PENNSYLVANIA)

Monet had a large garden at his country house in the French village of Giverny. He built an arched Japanese footbridge over the pond and filled the pond with water lilies. He spent 25 years sketching and painting the way light fell on the water and the flowers. He painted more than 200 pictures of water lilies!

Show Me the Light

When you mix a bunch of colors together, you sometimes end up with a muddy mess. Instead, try dabbing colors side by side. Now, stand back and let your eyes blend them. This is the technique Monet used.

The still water of a pond reflects light, almost like a mirror, but light also shines through it. The water lilies help the viewer see the surface of the water.

There are no blacks or grays. The shadows come from colors.

Water lilies are flowers that grow in water.

Edgar Degas
1834-1917

Edgar Degas is known for his images of ballet dancers. He created more than 1,500 paintings, drawings, prints, and sculptures of dancers. Like his friend Manet, Degas was born in Paris, France, to a rich family and was training to be a lawyer but quit to go to art school. His father wasn't happy with his choice.

In motion

In Degas's pictures, most of his dancers are not on stage. They are waiting in the wings, rehearsing, stretching, or resting. He gives the viewer glimpses of backstage, practice rooms, and the hours and hours of hard work.

Degas was fascinated by movement. He didn't like stiff, posed paintings. Instead of paint, he often used soft **pastels**, blurring the edges to suggest motion. Pastels are sticks of powdered pigment. They are applied dry in thick strokes and then blended on the paper to soften the tones. With swift lines, Degas captured the dancers' many gestures, stretches, and twirls.

A kind-of Impressionist

Unlike the other Impressionists, Degas did not paint outside. He felt an artist should control light, not be its servant. He often worked from memory. He continued to use black in his paintings, even though the other Impressionists rejected the color as unnatural.

Degas liked the off-center compositions of Japanese woodblock prints. His paintings and pastels sometimes look like photographs, because figures are **cropped**, or cut off, by the edge of the picture.

Art is not what you see, but what you make others see.

Created by hand

Later in life, Degas became a sculptor because his eyesight was failing. He sculpted mostly dancers and horses, and all were small in size. One of his most famous sculptures, *Little Fourteen-Year-Old Dancer*, is dressed in a real cloth tutu. Degas added real hair that he braided and tied with a ribbon.

The mirror shows us what's happening on the side of the room that is cropped.

The Dance Class

(1874, OIL ON CANVAS, THE METROPOLITAN MUSEUM OF ART IN NEW YORK, NEW YORK)

This painting captures a "moment in time." Like many of the dancers in Degas's art, these ballerinas are not performing. It's as if we are in the room with them, watching their dance class.

Some dancers have their backs turned and all of them are ignoring us, which adds to the feeling that we are peeking. The class is not glamorous but hard work. The dance master is in the center of the picture. He inspects the dancer's form. During this time period, almost all ballet dancers were of the working class. Competitive young dancers wait with their mothers in the back.

Behind the Scenes

Shhh! Dance class is in session. Look around Degas's painting to see what's happening.

- Why is the dance master focused on one girl? How is he feeling?
- Is there music playing? What kind?
- Notice how the right side of the room is cut off. What aren't we seeing?
- Is this the beginning of the class or the end?

The picture is painted mostly with earth colors, but the the flowers in the girls' hair and the sashes show accents of bright colors. Degas used loose brushstrokes and dabs of color.

The empty space at the bottom contrasts with the crowd of dancers at the top.

I will astonish Paris with an apple!

Paul Cézanne
1839-1906

Cézanne became friends with many of the Impressionist painters of the time, but he didn't want to paint like they did. He wasn't interested in showing a moment in time and the effect of light. He wanted to explore the structure of objects.

Paul Cézanne showed the art world a new way of seeing the objects around them. Cézanne was born in Aix-en-Provence, in the south of France, to a wealthy family. His father was a banker, and he was expected to be a banker, too. His father was very angry when Paul announced, after two years of law school, that he wanted to be an artist. His best friend, the writer Émile Zola, told Cézanne he couldn't let his father stop him. Finally, his mother convinced his father to let him try art.

A little help from my friend

Cézanne moved to Paris, but no one would exhibit his work. His paintings were very dark and dramatic. Instead of using a brush, he'd often apply the paint thickly with a **palette knife**. A fellow artist named Camille Pissarro encouraged him to paint outside in the sunlight. Cézanne's art changed. He painted with brighter colors and shorter brushstrokes.

Shapes in a bowl

Cézanne is best known for his **still lifes**. Still lifes are close-up paintings of items that do not move. Still lifes can be of fruits, vegetables, flowers, bottles, or bowls. You can even make still lifes of your stuffed animals, paper clips, and candy! Cézanne used still lifes to study the basic shapes of everyday objects. He saw everything as a cylinder, cone, sphere, or cube.

Set Up a Still Life

When drawing or painting a still life, don't just throw a bunch of fruit in a bowl or flowers in a vase. Note the shape, color, and texture of all your items and carefully arrange them into a well-balanced composition. Try placing a tablecloth or piece of fabric under your still life arrangement to add pattern or additional color.

Paint what you find

Cézanne liked the challenge of creating a great painting using only items he found around his house. He painted over 100 still lifes. Unfortunately, his work was largely unknown and rejected until he was quite old, and he thought he was a failure for most of his life. At age 67, while outside working on a canvas, a thunderstorm rolled in. He refused to stop. Later, he was found unconscious on the ground and died at home from pneumonia.

Not done yet

Very few of Cézanne's paintings are signed. To him, a signature meant a painting was complete. Every time he came back to a still life, he noticed something new or that the smallest thing had changed. He wanted to paint exactly what he saw, so he'd work some more on the painting.

Cézanne took so long on each painting that the fruit he was using often rotted before he finished, and he'd have to get new fruit.

Cézanne often painted apples because he liked their simple, spherical shape. None of the apples are just one color. He used many shades of red, yellow, and green.

Curtain, Jug, and Bowl of Fruit

(1894, OIL ON CANVAS, PRIVATE COLLECTION)

The fruit in this still life looks as if it spilled randomly from the bowl onto the white cloth. Not so. Cézanne spent a lot of time positioning each apple and pear and figuring out the folds of the cloth. He also spent a lot of time painting each piece of fruit. If you look closely, you can see that, like in nature, each apple is slightly different from the next.

He used complementary colors for the shadows. The bright colors of the fruit contrast with the gray background.

Pierre-Auguste Renoir
1841–1919

Like many artists, Renoir did not become famous until after he died—and then he became super-famous! Renoir was born in Limoges, France, but he grew up in Paris, not far from the famous art museum the Louvre. He would visit often to look at the paintings and sculptures. At 13, he took a job painting flowers on porcelain to help his father, who was a poor tailor, make money. He learned how to paint with a steady but delicate hand.

He began to study art when he was 17. His teacher taught in the old-fashioned style, emphasizing historical or religious scenes painted with dark colors. One day, another student named Claude Monet invited Renoir to join him in painting outside. Renoir was surprised by how much he loved it. Renoir and Monet had similar ways of painting, and they often painted side by side "en plein air." They became good friends and often shared food when they had no money.

Happy faces, happy places

Renoir is known as "the painter of happiness." He painted beautiful people relaxing and having fun. He thought paintings should make the viewer happy, and he felt that the people on his canvas should look happy as well. Renoir was an Impressionist. He painted with bright colors in wide strokes to give the appearance of light when seen from a distance.

Later in life, Renoir came down with serious arthritis, which deformed his hands. He couldn't hold a brush. The only way he could paint was to tie the paintbrush to his arm.

Renoir used his friends as models. The man with the straw hat on the left was the son of the owner of the restaurant. The woman cooing at her little dog was Renoir's girlfriend, whom he later married.

The Luncheon of the Boating Party at Bougival

(1880-1881, OIL ON CANVAS, PHILLIPS COLLECTION IN WASHINGTON, D.C.)

This famous, joyful scene shows a summer boating party finishing their meal on a terrace overlooking the Seine River in Paris. Renoir captures their friendship through their relaxed poses and the way they gather and gossip together. Renoir also captures their happiness. The people glow, and the glasses, dishes, and fruit on the table sparkle. There is no symbolism in this painting. Renoir purely meant to show a "slice of life," and the painting looks like a just-snapped photograph.

Sunlight Scratch Art

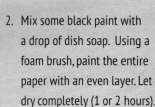

You Need:

- Heavy paper
- Oil pastels or crayons (yellow, orange, red, pink)
- Black tempera paint
- Liquid dish soap
- Foam brush
- Pointed wooden stick or toothpick

You Create:

1. Cover the entire paper with a thick layer of pastel or crayon in different "sunny" colors. Do not leave any white space.

2. Mix some black paint with a drop of dish soap. Using a foam brush, paint the entire paper with an even layer. Let dry completely (1 or 2 hours).

3. With the tip of your pointy object, scrape a simple picture. The bright color from underneath will shine through, giving the effect of shimmering sunlight.

Study the people in the painting. Only two are actually looking at one another. Who are they?

Renoir used a palette of rainbow colors. He painted shadows bright blue and lavender instead of black.

Mary Cassatt
1844-1926

Cassatt was active in the women's suffrage movement in America. She donated the money she made at special art shows to help pass the law granting women the right to vote.

Mary Cassatt was one of the first women to become a serious artist when very few women were artists or even had professions at all. Born near Pittsburgh, Pennsylvania, Mary and her wealthy family moved to Paris and Germany for several years when she was seven. Her parents took her to art museums and galleries, igniting her love of art. When they returned to the United States, her father felt Mary should get married, stay home, and raise children. Mary only wanted to paint.

Mary convinced her father to send her to the Pennsylvania Academy of the Fine Arts. At that time, the few women in art school weren't allowed into the model drawing classes since sometimes models took off their clothes—so they began to model for themselves! These women were determined to learn how to draw the human body. Mary was one of them. She wanted to be independent and pursue her art.

Off to Paris

In the late 1800s, Cassatt moved to Paris. The art school in Paris would not accept women, so Cassatt spent her time in the museums, copying the Old Masters. Not long after she arrived, one of her paintings was shown at the **Salon**. This was a huge deal. The Salon accepted few new artists and even fewer women.

What was the Salon?

Every one or two years, the French Academy held a big **exhibition**, or art show, of thousands of new paintings. This show was called the Salon. A selection committee decided which artists made it into the Salon. If the Salon invited you to exhibit, you could then show your work in museums and public galleries. If you were rejected . . . forget it. Rejected paintings were even stamped with a big "R" on the back, which an artist had to find a way to cover up if he or she ever hoped to sell the painting.

The Salon didn't like new ideas and new techniques. By 1863, thousands of painters were being rejected. The ruler of France, Napoleon III, asked to see the rejected paintings. He liked a lot of them! He ordered that another exhibition be set up and called it the "Salon des Refusés," which means "Salon of the Refused." Many famous Impressionist painters got their start there.

Best friends

Cassatt became close friends with Edgar Degas, who introduced her to the other Impressionists. She liked their style and started using soft, sweeping brushstrokes, bright colors, and pastels. Cassatt and Degas became such good friends that when an Impressionist exhibition wouldn't include his work, she withdrew hers, too.

A people person

Cassatt is known for painting women and children. She painted young mothers bathing, sewing, and comforting their children. Her approach was unique in that it showed the mother-child bond in a non-religious way. She wanted to show their deep connection and their emotions.

Cassatt used bold outlines and delicate, clear colors. The orange-red flowers pop against the white and light blue of the mother and daughter's clothing.

The "V" pattern of the lines on the mother's dress draws the focus to her lap and her child.

Where Are All the Women Artists?

Mary Cassatt hated being called a "woman artist" and wished she'd be called simply "an artist." For the longest time, art was considered only a hobby for women. Very few art schools and exhibitions accepted women until the 1800s. While there were some women artists, dating as far back as pottery painting in ancient Greece and tapestry weaving in medieval times, it wasn't until the late 1900s that the art world began to celebrate and promote women.

Beside Cassatt, other famous female artists you may want to learn about include **Berthe Morisot, Grandma Moses, Frida Kahlo, Georgia O'Keefe, Faith Ringgold, Helen Frankenthaler, Louise Nevelson**, and **Cindy Sherman**. The National Museum of Women in the Arts in Washington, D.C., is devoted entirely to women artists, and you can go online to check out its collections.

Young Mother Sewing

(1900, OIL ON CANVAS, THE METROPOLITAN MUSEUM OF ART, NEW YORK, NEW YORK)

We feel as if we are spying on a private, quiet moment in this portrait. The mother is focused on her sewing, as her child leans easily against her knee. The comfortable positions of their bodies, so in tune with one another, show their closeness. They are both absorbed in their life at home, turning their backs to the dark green world outside the window. Cassatt painted everyday family activities because she felt they were special by not being special.

The child's rosy cheeks makes her appear as if she has just run in.

Guess what? The woman and child are not mother and daughter. They are not even related. They are models hired by Cassatt.

When Is Flat Not Flat?

How do artists make objects painted on a flat piece of paper it look real and 3-D? They use perspective. Perspective tricks your eyes.

The basic idea of perspective is:

If an object is close to you, draw it bigger.

If an object is far from you, draw it smaller.

Here is a road with three trees. Which tree looks biggest? The one closest to you. In real life, the trees would be the about same size. Two are drawn smaller in the picture, so you know they are far away.

Artists use a **horizon line**. This is an imaginary line across the page where the sky and earth meet.

The road in this picture goes back and seems to disappear at a single point. This imaginary point on the horizon line is called the **vanishing point**.

Objects become smaller and smaller the closer they are to the horizon line. And then they completely disappear at the vanishing point.

Vanishing point

Horizon line

Background

Middleground

Foreground

Let's draw a house in perspective!

If you look at a house from the front it looks like this:

But you don't live in a flat house, do you?

If you look at a house from an angle, it looks like this:

Let's start with a piece of paper, a pencil with an eraser, and a ruler. Use your ruler to draw every line!

As explorer Christopher Columbus discovered centuries ago, our world is not flat. Using these perspective hints will help make your art appear real. Some viewers may be so tricked that they'll reach out to touch the 3-D objects in your drawing!

	Size objects appear	Amount of detail
Foreground	Large	A lot
Middle ground	Medium	Medium
Background	Small	Very little

Step 1: Lightly draw a horizontal line across the center of your paper. This is the horizon line. Draw an x on the line towards the right side. The X is the vanishing point.

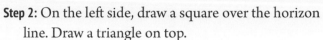

Step 2: On the left side, draw a square over the horizon line. Draw a triangle on top.

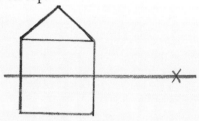

Step 3: Using your ruler, draw lines connecting the two right-side corners of the square and the top point of the triangle to the x.

Step 4: Halfway along the new triangle you've created, draw a vertical line. This is the backside of your house.

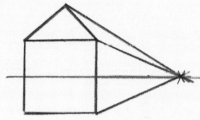

Step 5: Erase all the lines you don't need and color in your house.

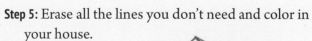

Auguste Rodin
1840-1917

Broken nose

Rodin began making sculptures. He studied Michelangelo's work, as well as ancient Greek and Roman sculpture. Unlike Classical sculptors, who created ideal beauties, Rodin tried to show people the way they really were. One of his first statues was of an ugly old boxer that he called *Man with a Broken Nose*. The Salon in Paris rejected it twice. Years later, it was accepted.

A person inside

Rodin often took years to make one sculpture. He sometimes sculpted more than a dozen heads in one day, then trashed them all before he went to bed. He worked hard to make his sculpture look alive. When he exhibited his first important sculpture, it was so realistic, people thought there was a live model inside it!

Auguste Rodin is known as a pioneer of modern sculpture. Rodin was born in Paris, France. He had a difficult time in school, so he'd draw pictures instead of doing his work. At age 14, he entered a school of decorative arts and then got a job doing decorative stonework. But Rodin wanted to be an artist.

He applied to the most famous art school in Paris three times. They rejected him three times. When he was 22, he was so upset when his sister died that he decided to give up art and become a monk. The Father Superior told him he was making the wrong choice. He convinced Rodin to go back into the world and be an artist.

Two ways to sculpt

Since the beginning of time, there have been two basic ways to make sculpture. Rodin used both.

1) The artist carves, chips, or takes away from a block of material until the sculpture "appears."

2) The artist "builds up" the sculpture using wire and clay. To make the sculpture last a long time and not crack, metal is poured into a clay mold and forms the same shape as the clay.

The Thinker

(1903, BRONZE, RODIN MUSEUM IN PARIS, FRANCE)

One of the most famous sculptures of all time, *The Thinker* was originally part of a commission by the French government for a museum of decorative arts in Paris. Rodin was hired to sculpt a great set of doors based on the epic poem *The Divine Comedy* by Dante. He called the piece *The Gates of Hell.* At the top is the figure of Dante bent over in thought, reflecting on hell below. After Rodin completed the doors, he turned this one figure into a larger sculpture called *The Thinker.* With its strength and realism, the statue has become a symbol of freedom and knowledge.

The Thinker was modeled in clay then cast in bronze. While Rodin was alive he did many castings of the statue, and since his death many more have been made.

Some Places to See *The Thinker* in the United States

Adrian College, Adrian, Michigan

Detroit Institute of Arts, Detroit, Michigan

Cleveland Museum of Art, Cleveland, Ohio

California Palace of the Legion of Honor, San Francisco

Columbia University, New York, New York

Stanford University, Stanford, California

Norton Simon Museum, Pasadena, California

Rodin Museum, Philadelphia, Pennsylvania

Baltimore Museum of Art, Baltimore, Maryland

Trinity University, San Antonio, Texas

Nelson-Atkins Museum of Art, Kansas City, Missouri

University of Louisville, Louisville, Kentucky (the first cast made from the original sculpture)

At the end of his life, Rodin lived in a hotel in Paris that was scheduled to be torn down. He didn't want to leave, so he made a deal. When he died, the French government would inherit all his art, and he got to stay.

Nothing makes me so happy as to observe nature and to paint what I see.

Henri Rousseau is famous today for his enchanting and mysterious paintings, but while he was alive, his art was constantly rejected and mocked. Born in Laval, France, Rousseau didn't do well in school and often got into trouble. Years later, he said he wished someone had noticed that he was good at art and sent him to art school. No one ever did. Everything Rousseau learned about art, he taught himself.

Sticks and stones

Rousseau's nickname was "Le Douanier," which means "customs officer" in French. He collected tolls at one of the gates in Paris and painted only in his free time. An outsider from the start, he joined the "Salon of the Independents," a group of artists who exhibited their work without the approval of the official Salon. Critics laughed at his self-taught style. They said it was too

simple looking. They said a lot of other very mean things. But other artists thought his paintings had a strange, dream-like quality. They told him to keep on painting.

Wide world

In 1889, the World's Fair came to Paris with exhibits from all over the world. At that time, you couldn't turn on the TV or surf the Internet to see pictures and videos from far-off places. Rousseau first realized how exotic and large the world was at the World's Fair. He wanted to travel, but instead, he began to paint his imagined adventures in faraway lands.

Even though he'd never been to a jungle, Rousseau loved making tropical pictures. He'd sketch in local parks and zoos. He used pictures from magazines. People laughed at his paintings because they looked unreal. Rousseau kept on painting them.

Primitive painter

Rousseau is grouped with the **Post-Impressionist** artists, who broke free from the naturalism of Impressionism, but he is also called a **primitive** or **naïve** painter. His style was child-like, often resembling illustrations in a storybook. Rousseau worked on his canvases slowly, inch by inch. During his life he had only one solo exhibition, but even then, he wasn't very successful. Today, his paintings hang in major museums worldwide.

Sometimes the images he painted scared Rousseau, and he had to poke his head out his studio window for a calming gulp of air.

In the Jungle

Just like Rousseau, you don't need to visit a jungle to make great jungle art.

You Need:

- Green construction paper
- White drawing paper
- Markers or paint/brushes
- Scissors
- Glue stick

You Create:

1. Using either colored markers or paint, draw a jungle animal on the white paper. How about a tiger, snake, hippo, monkey, parrot, or gorilla?

2. Now cut leaves from the green construction paper. Make your leaves all different shapes and sizes.

3. Using your glue stick, attach the leaves to the white paper to create your jungle. Be sure your leaves **overlap**. Have the leaves cover up parts of your jungle animal.

4. You can add flowers and tall grass with markers.

Tiger in a Tropical Storm
also known as
Surprised!

(1891, OIL ON CANVAS, NATIONAL GALLERY IN LONDON, ENGLAND)

This was the first of Rousseau's many jungle paintings. Lit up by a flash of lightening, a tiger is ready to pounce on its unseen prey—maybe even a human explorer! Rousseau first exhibited it under the title *Surprised!* The slanting rain and the wind whipping through the tall grass show the intensity of the storm.

The many shades of green show the lushness of the jungle leaves. How many different greens can you find?

Some of these plants aren't really jungle plants but houseplants that he used as "models."

Rousseau used glowing colors, strong shadows, and dramatic shading.

I shut my eyes in order to see.

Paul Gauguin
1848-1903

Color Surprise

You Need:

- Bright colors of paint
- Brushes
- Large piece of paper
- Pencil

You Create:

1. Before you put your brush to your paper, think of an outdoor scene you want to paint, for example, a day at the beach, dogs playing in the park, or a bear in the forest. You can lightly sketch the scene first with pencil or jump in with paint.

2. As you work, paint things the **opposite color** of how they really appear. Make the sky green, the sand blue, or the bear purple. Paint your colors solid and flat like Gauguin did.

Paul Gauguin traveled the world, searching for adventure and beauty, then painted what he experienced. Born in Paris, he spent much of his childhood in Peru. Never one to stay still, Gauguin joined the merchant marines as a teenager and sailed around the world. When he returned, he became a successful stockbroker in Paris. He spent a lot of money buying paintings by Monet and other artists who were showing their work at that time. Gauguin took up painting as a weekend hobby. Soon, he realized that all he wanted to do was paint.

Far, far away

Gauguin gave up his job to paint full-time. He also gave up his wife and five children. He turned his back on everything and everyone. He was convinced that he needed to live a simpler life to create his best work. He traveled to the Caribbean island of Martinique and even worked on building the Panama Canal. Then, he moved in with painter Vincent Van Gogh in the south of France. That didn't go well. They had a major fight, and Gauguin left. He still couldn't find the perfect place to paint.

Island paradise

In 1891, Gauguin moved by himself to the island of Tahiti. Tahiti is in the middle of the Pacific Ocean between South America and Australia. Gauguin was convinced that people in Europe were mean and sneaky. He liked the directness and spirit in Tahiti. He wanted to live in harmony with nature.

Color my world

In Tahiti, a tropical island covered in rainforest, Gauguin's art changed. He painted the world around him but he added his imagination to the mix. He wanted to combine dream with reality to create an enchanted

Nave Nave Moe

(1894, OIL ON CANVAS, THE HERMITAGE MUSEUM IN ST. PETERSBURG, RUSSIA)

The title of this painting means "Sacred Spring, Sweet Dreams" in the Tahitian language.
Gauquin's art was very much influenced by his surroundings. He painted this soon after he
arrived in Tahiti, capturing the primitive beauty of the people and the island.

His people look child-like to show the uncomplicated lives of the natives.

All his figures have clear outlines.

He used flat areas of color instead of dabs and streaks.

He chose loud colors, with shocking color contrasts.

The people of Tahiti didn't much like Gauguin.

world. He found inspiration in the bold colors and flat
shapes of Tahitian tribal art. He developed a new style
with strong outlines filled with bright, flat colors—much
more intense than those found in nature. For example, he
painted a dog red, the sky yellow, or a tree blue.

Vincent Van Gogh
1853-1890

Looking at the stars always makes me dream.

Today Vincent Van Gogh's paintings sell for millions of dollars, but when he was alive, he was a starving artist who only sold one painting! Van Gogh was born in the Netherlands, and his father was a minister. He got bad grades in school and dropped out at age 14. He tried many different jobs—teacher, preacher, bookstore clerk—and failed at all of them. At age 27, he decided to be a painter. He taught himself by copying works of famous artists such as Rembrandt. Van Gogh's early paintings were very dark and sad. No one liked them. No one bought them.

On to Paris

Van Gogh moved to Paris, and the colors he used became brighter. He liked to use the paint straight from the tube, so the color was strong. He had intense moods—sometimes he was very happy and sometimes very sad—and he used color to show his feelings. He was influenced by Japanese woodblock prints. He liked their simple design, flat areas of color, and absence of shadows. All this can be seen in his own work. He often made one painting per day. He painted almost 2,000 paintings in ten years, yet he only sold one while he was alive.

Often, Van Gogh would work day and night without stopping. To see at night, he attached lighted candles around the brim of his straw hat!

A little sun

He moved from Paris to the South of France to paint. He felt the bright colors and sunshine there would inspire him. He rented a house and invited his friend Paul Gauguin to join him there. They did not live together well and argued all the time. After two months, Gauguin left. Throughout his life, Van Gogh suffered from mental illness and depression, which means he was very, very sad. He had to be treated at a mental hospital. At age 37, he shot and killed himself. After his death, his brother Theo, an art dealer and his best friend, organized exhibitions and finally sold Van Gogh's work.

He's a . . .

Van Gogh is sometimes called a Post-Impressionist painter—but his style never belonged to any movement. Mainly, he tried to express emotions through his art.

All 11 twinkling stars are in the correct spots in the sky!

The huge sky makes the village look tiny. The lines and angles of the houses contrast with the curves in the sky.

The Starry Night

(1889, OIL ON CANVAS, THE MUSEUM OF MODERN ART IN NEW YORK, NEW YORK)

Van Gogh painted *The Starry Night* while at a mental hospital, and a lot of people think it's his best work. The dramatic night sky filled with swirling shapes shows his troubled mind. Van Gogh did not paint it outdoors. The scene is partially the view out his hospital window and partially imagined. Van Gogh never told anyone what the picture meant. Do you have any ideas?

The twisting cypress trees and the church spire connect earth with the heavens.

The swirling brushstrokes give the painting movement. The thick layers of paint, called **impasto**, show how fast Van Gogh worked.

The Ear Story

It's hard to say which of the many stories told about Van Gogh's ear is true, since only Van Gogh and Paul Gauguin were there that night. One story goes that Van Gogh and Gauguin had a horrible fight in a café. Van Gogh chased Gauguin down an alley and pulled out a razor. Gauguin taunted him and Van Gogh backed down, but then he went home and used the razor to slice off the lobe of his left ear. He wrapped the earlobe in a handkerchief and took it to his friend Rachel and said, "Guard this object carefully." She fainted. Van Gogh returned home and nearly bled to death in his bed. Another story has the two artists arguing at home, Gauguin storming out, and Van Gogh slicing off his ear lobe and leaving the package for Rachel. In yet another story, Gauguin told Van Gogh outside the café that he was leaving Arles, and Van Gogh became so upset that he threw a wine glass at Gauguin. Gauguin pulled out his sword and, either on purpose or by accident in the darkness, sliced off Van Gogh's ear lobe. In any case, Van Gogh recovered then painted his famous *Self-Portrait with Bandaged Ear.*

Georges Seurat
1859-1891

From the very beginning, Georges Seurat wanted his art to be completely original. He didn't want to copy the Old Masters. He didn't want to paint like the artists around him, so he set about inventing a new way of painting with color. Born in Paris, Seurat attended the École des Beaux-Arts, the most famous art school in France. When he started his own studio, he drew mostly in only black and white for two years to better understand **tone**. Tone is the lightness or darkness of a color. One day, at an art show, he saw the work of the Impressionists. He liked their use of color and how they captured light, but he thought he could do it better. Much better.

Some say they see poetry in my paintings; I see only science.

Dot, dot, dot

At that time, most painters mixed their paints on a palette. Not Seurat. He dipped a small brush directly into each tube of paint and then "pointed" it right onto the canvas. He discovered that if you put dots of different colors next to one another, they blend together in your eyes when you stand back from the canvas. For example, if he put dabs of red next to dabs of yellow, at a distance, that area would appear orange. Browns and golds were formed by placing dots of red, blue, and orange next to one another.

Seurat made paintings from millions of tiny dots or dabs of paint placed very close together. Seurat called them "points of paint," and his new way of painting was called **Pointillism**.

Get to the point

Seurat did not paint outdoors, although he enjoyed creating pictures of people by rivers. He'd sketch outside, then return to his studio to paint. His pointillist paintings took years to finish, because he was very careful where he placed each dot. Seurat is called a **"Neo-Impressionist,"** or "New Impressionist," since his technique was very scientific and precise. Before having a chance to create many paintings, he died suddenly from a disease called diphtheria when he was only 32.

A Sunday on the Grande Jatte

(1884–86, OIL ON CANVAS, THE ART INSTITUTE OF CHICAGO IN ILLINOIS)

This famous pointillist painting shows people in Paris enjoying a beautiful summer Sunday on a small island in the Seine River. Boating was very fashionable then, as you can see by the many boats in the river. People relax beneath shady trees and take walks in the grass. Seurat worked on this painting for two years, perfecting the dot-color combinations. Millions of color dots fill this huge painting!

You can see the influence of Egyptian art, which Seurat studied, in the way many of his figures are stiff and in profile.

The painting is **static**, as if everyone was told to freeze in place. There's a silent, unmoving quality.

Search and Find

A lot of activity is happening in this park. Can you find the following?

- 3 dogs
- 1 monkey on a leash
- 1 man playing a horn
- 1 man smoking a pipe
- 2 soldiers
- 1 pink butterfly
- 1 cane

Seurat painted his own frame. He changed the colors in different sections of the frame so that they would be **complementary** to the colors next to them in the painting.

Seurat discovered that tiny dots of orange scattered among the other colors gave the impression of sparkling sunlight.

Why is there a monkey in the park? Capuchin monkeys were fashionable pets in Paris in the 1880s.

Gustav Klimt
1862-1918

Gustav Klimt was a master of eye-popping pattern and metallic color. Klimt's father was a gold engraver in Vienna, Austria, who taught his son how to work with gold. Klimt won a scholarship to art school. When he finished, he and his brother started a business painting murals on walls and ceilings for mansions, theaters, and universities.

Golden phase

Klimt switched from murals to painting on canvases. He was inspired by Byzantine mosaics from the Medieval Period, which used tiny pieces of colored glass, shiny stones, gold, and silver to make images and patterns. Klimt used a lot of gold and metallic paint in his art, and this was called his "golden phase."

Something new

Klimt was part of a group of artists in Vienna who were tired of the realistic art that had been made for hundreds of years. They believed that art was everywhere, and decorative crafts were just as important as fine art. They wanted their art to symbolize something beyond what appeared on the canvas. They wanted to use bright colors. They wanted to use swirling, flowing lines. They called their style **Art Nouveau**, or "New Art."

Pick a pattern

Klimt loved patterns. He would repeat shapes, lines, or colors in an arrangement. Can you list all the places you see decorative patterns? Here's a hint—fabrics, bedding, furniture, jewelry, and dishes.

Klimt is one of many artists who used **gold leaf** in his pictures. These leaves don't grow on golden trees! Gold leaf is gold that has been hammered into very, very thin sheets.

The Kiss

(1907-1908, OIL ON CANVAS WITH GOLD AND SILVER
LEAF, ÖSTERREICHISCHE GALERIE BELVEDERE IN
VIENNA, AUSTRIA)

This glowing painting of a man and woman is filled with
emotion. The man kisses the woman's cheek as if it is their
last kiss—or maybe, it's their first. The focus is on their
heads and faces. Everything else is a swirl of pattern. They
appear separate yet also united in their tight embrace.

The man's gown and the woman's gown have
different geometric patterns. What shapes do
you see in each?

Pattern Maker

To make a pattern, start with one shape. For example,
draw a circle.

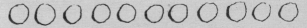

Now draw a row of circles all the same size.

Next add more rows under your first row, all of the same circle.

Color the first circle red and the second circle blue, then the third
circle red and the fourth circle blue. Keep alternating the colors. You
have a pattern!

The pattern in the
carpet of jewel-tone
flowers has the feeling
of a Byzantine mosaic.

The painting is almost entirely gold, except for the faces
of the man and the woman. Klimt scraped decorative
lines directly into the gold leaf.

Edvard Munch
1863-1944

Edvard Munch had a sad childhood, and that sadness lived on in his art. He was born in Loten, Norway, but moved with his family to the city of Oslo. When he was a child, his mother and sister died of tuberculosis, and another sister was sent away to a mental institution. His father was an intensely religious man who would shut himself away to pray for the entire day. Often sick, Edvard spent his days drawing inside the family's apartment.

Munch went to art school in Oslo, then moved to Paris to paint. His first major work, *Sick Child*, dealt with his sister's death. It captured his sadness and guilt over watching her die.

Let it out

Munch displayed his feelings on his canvases. His style is called **Expressionism**, because the focus is not on how an object looks but on the artist's pure emotion. He wanted the viewer to feel his anger, fear, or sickness.

A tough life

Munch suffered from depression, often complained of hearing voices in his head, and was addicted to alcohol. During an especially dark time in his life, he painted a series of 22 paintings called *The Frieze of Life*. The paintings had titles such as *Melancholy, Jealousy, Despair, Anxiety,* and *The Scream*. The exhibition had to be pulled down after only one week because people found his art upsetting.

Munch showed emotion through intense colors. The orange sky clashes with the blue water.

The swirling landscape shows his turmoil.

The Scream

(1893, OIL, TEMPERA, AND PASTEL ON CARDBOARD, NATIONAL GALLERY OF NORWAY AND THE MUNCH MUSEUM IN OSLO, NORWAY)

The Scream is the ultimate in Expressionist art. We see a lonely man with a skull-like head. His mouth is open, and he's clutching his face in fear. The screaming man is Munch. He wrote in his diary that the image came from a time when he was walking with two friends at sunset, and he leaned against a rail to rest. Suddenly, he felt anxious. A scream exploded out of him that seemed to pass through all of nature. You can see the shockwaves of his terror rippling through the water and sky.

A pastel version of The Scream sold in 2012 for over $119 million.

Make a Face!

Do you often stick a smile on the faces you draw? Even if your people are always happy, drawing different expressions is a great way to show emotion in your art.

You Need:

- A mirror
- Paper
- Colored pencils

You Create:

1. Look in the mirror. Try making different expressions with your face. What do you look like when you're surprised? Angry? Scared? Sleepy? If you have a friend or parent nearby, have them try to guess which emotion your face is showing.

2. Now pick one emotion and make that face. On your paper, draw a large oval for your head. Add in your eyes, nose, and mouth. Look in the mirror. Is your mouth open or closed? Are your eyes wide or small?

3. Add details. Draw your eyebrows raised if you are surprised. Slant your eyebrows down if you are angry. Add tears if you are crying. Make your cheeks pink if you are embarrassed.

Henri de Toulouse-Lautrec
1864-1901

I paint things as they are. I don't comment. I record.

stopped growing. As an adult, he was barely five feet tall, with a normal body and very short legs. He found it difficult to walk and had to use a walking stick.

All-night party

Toulouse-Lautrec loved to go out at night in Paris. His artwork showed the nightclubs, waitresses, singers, and dancers. Toulouse-Lautrec would sketch all night in the dimly lit clubs and then paint the scenes in the morning in his studio. He was often drunk. He said he drank so much alcohol because he thought he was ugly. He died at the young age of 37.

Poster art

Toulouse-Lautrec was famous for his posters. He designed and printed posters to advertise Paris's dance halls. People loved his posters and would pull them off the walls as soon as they were hung to take them home. He used a method called **lithography** to make them. Lithography begins with a flat stone or metal surface. Some areas are made to attract ink and others are made to repel, or push away, ink. The artist doesn't carve the image but paints it on the surface.

Toulouse-Lautrec patterned his graphic posters after the style of Hokusai's woodblock prints. He used large areas of flat, bold color. He also outlined his figures sharply and never used shadows. Sometimes he'd print on cardboard, because he liked the background color.

Henri de Toulouse-Lautrec captured the carefree spirit of Paris at the end of the 1800s in his colorful, fun-loving posters. Born in Albi, France, Toulouse-Lautrec never had to worry about money during his life because his father and mother were a count and countess. He was often sick as a child and spent a lot of time painting and drawing. When he was 14, he broke his left leg. When he was 15, he broke his right leg. He had a bone disease, so his bones did not heal properly and his legs

How did artists in France in the 1800s discover Japanese woodblock prints by Hokusai? In 1856, a French painter was unwrapping porcelain that had been shipped from Japan. The wrapping paper had been ripped from a book of prints. The artist rushed to share them with his painter friends.

Moulin Rouge: La Goulue

(1891, COLOR LITHOGRAPH, INDIANAPOLIS MUSEUM OF ART IN INDIANA)

Henri de Toulouse-Lautrec made this nearly six-foot-tall poster to promote the dancer "La Goulue" (whose real name was Louise Weber) at the new Paris dance hall called the Moulin Rouge. She was well known for dancing the famous can-can. He printed about 3,000 copies, and in December 1891, the poster was plastered all over Paris. The other posters on the streets were filled with a lot of words, so the bold pictures of the Moulin Rouge poster really stood out. Afterward, everyone was talking about the new artist who had created it.

Mad about Ads

Henri de Toulouse-Lautrec made advertising into a fine art. Now you can design your own poster advertisement.

You Need:

- Poster-size paper or board
- Pencil
- Markers or paint

You Create:

1. Think of something real or imaginary to advertise on your poster. For example, a circus, a pet adoption, a book fair, a concert, a relative coming to visit, or a magic show. Think of a catchy phrase, such as "Circus Coming to Town!" or "Presto Change-O!"

2. Using a pencil, map out your poster by sketching the words and the central image. For a circus, you might draw a clown. For a magic show, you might draw a rabbit in a hat. Keep everything simple and graphic.

3. Make your words and pictures pop by adding bold color with markers or paint.

The audience is shown in black silhouettes, so we focus on the dancer.

The repetition of "Moulin Rouge" draws our eye down to the dancer and her white petticoats.

Toulouse-Lautrec used warm colors—red, yellow, and orange.

This was one of the earliest "celebrity" posters to promote a famous performer. Think about movie and sports posters now. Toulouse-Lautrec really started something!

Where Is Art?

Museums

Most of the art shown in this book is housed in an **art museum**. An art museum is a special place built to display and view art. But a museum is much more than a place to hang paintings . . .

Museums hold the right temperature

It can't be too hot or cold, too damp or dry, inside a museum. If the temperature isn't just right, paint can crack or peel. One reason some ancient art has lasted for so long is that it was preserved in cool caves or dry deserts.

Museums make choices

The art displayed in each museum is chosen by a **curator.** A curator is a specially trained person who chooses the artwork and decides how it is displayed.

Museums keep the art looking good

Museums hire **conservators** to clean and restore paintings so that years from now, they will look just-painted. **Art preservation** is very slow and detailed work. Conservators remove dirt and old varnish and repair cracking paint. They often use X-rays and infrared reflectography to explore beneath the layers of paint. They can learn how the artist worked, the types of brushstrokes he or she used, and even see early sketches done under the paint.

Museums have special rooms

Art museums are often divided into **galleries** or **collections**. Galleries help to group similar works together. For example, a museum may have an Impressionism Gallery, an Ancient Egyptian Gallery, or a collection of Medieval Art.

Museums teach

Visiting a museum is not about quietly staring at art. Today, many museums offer special programs for kids. There are exhibits you can touch, treasure hunts, family tours, and art camps.

Other places to see art

Most cities have **art galleries**. Unlike a museum, private art galleries are a business. While you are welcome to walk around and look at the art for free, the owner or the gallery hopes to sell the art displayed on the walls. Many galleries feature different **shows**, which highlight the work of one artist or a group of artists.

Artists often have **art exhibitions** where they show their art. Exhibitions can be in a museum, a gallery, at a fair, in a school or a church, at a local coffee shop, or at an art festival. Even your school may host an art exhibition.

There are many **online sites** where you can look at art. Some big museums let you view their virtual collections and click through the paintings, as if you were walking through the halls of the museum. Other sites act like online catalogues, with some selling the work and some purely educational.

"Do I hear two million?"

Important works of art are often sold at an **art auction**. The two most famous art auction houses are Christie's and Sotheby's. At an auction, a work of art is sold to the highest bidder, or the person who is willing to pay the most money.

Here's how an auction works:

If you buy a chocolate bar in a candy store, you pay the price listed on the chocolate. If there were an auction for the chocolate bar, the store owner would gather all the people interested in buying that one special chocolate bar. She would announce an opening **bid**, or price, let's say 50¢. If you feel okay paying more, you would increase the bid to 60¢. Maybe the boy next to you raises the bid to 75¢, and the man behind him goes up to 90¢. People drop out of an auction when the price gets too high. Now it's just you and the boy left. Are you willing to spend 95¢ on the chocolate? If you are and he isn't, then the candy bar is yours for that price. Art auctions work the same way.

Try it

Why not have your own art exhibition? Gather your friends and display your art inside someone's house. Make posters and invite your neighbors and friends. Or have an auction of your artwork. Adults can bid real money that you could donate to a charity—or you could give your friends candies or chips to use as fake money.

Henri Matisse
1869-1954

Called the "King of Color," Henri Matisse was known for his bold use of bright color. Matisse was born in a small town in northern France, and his parents owned a general store. He planned on becoming a lawyer, but he got very sick at age 20. While he was in bed getting better, his mother bought him a box of paints. He discovered that he loved painting. He gave up law, moved to Paris, and trained to become an artist.

Color my world

Matisse was intrigued by the power of color. Seeing different colors makes us feel different emotions, such as calmness, anger, or happiness. That's why hospital walls are painted soothing colors. When Matisse started painting, new colors and pigments were being created. The paint was premixed and not too expensive, allowing Matisse to experiment with color. He painted with few lines and only a few colors. Matisse felt that the simpler the color, the stronger it becomes.

Creativity takes courage.

Wild and crazy

When Matisse and several other painters exhibited their work in 1905, a critic said they were like *fauves*, which means "wild beasts." The name **Fauves** stuck for artists who used a lot of bright, bold colors to express their emotions. Matisse was the leader of the Fauves. He wanted to get rid of everything on the canvas that was not color.

Making the cut

Matisse painted until the end of his life, even when he was in a wheelchair and very sick. When he was too weak to paint at an easel, he created "paper cuts" by cutting out shapes from colored paper with scissors. He then collaged them into pictures. **Collage** comes from the French word *coller*, which means "to paste or glue." Matisse called his technique of making collages "drawing with scissors."

In 1961, Matisse's painting *Le Bateau (The Sailboat)* was displayed at the Museum of Modern Art in New York City. Forty-seven days later, someone realized it had been mistakenly hung upside down!

Painting with Scissors

Cutout collages look easy to make, but it's hard work to arrange the shapes and colors to create the most interesting picture.

You Need:

- Colored construction paper
- Scissors
- Glue stick

You Create:

1. Choose three or four colors of construction paper that you feel go together. Like Matisse, use your scissors to cut shapes directly into the paper. Try some spirals, zigzags, and curves, too. Save both your positive and negative shapes.

2. Wait until you have a pile of cutout shapes, then begin to arrange them on a large sheet of paper. Don't glue any down now, or you won't be able to move them around. Use only the shapes that you feel work best together, and put the extras in a pile on the side. Try overlapping and layering some shapes.

3. When you are happy with your design, glue down the shapes.

Pierrot's Funeral

(STENCIL PRINT, PLATE 10 OF THE ILLUSTRATED BOOK "JAZZ" BY H. MATISSE, 1947, HERBERT F. JOHNSON MUSEUM OF ART, CORNELL UNIVERSITY, IN ITHACA, NEW YORK, OR STANFORD UNIVERSITY LIBRARY IN PALO ALTO, CALIFORNIA*)

Jazz is the title of an illustrated book by Henri Matisse which includes 20 reproductions of his cutouts. *Pierrot's Funeral* is number ten. The portfolio is not about jazz music. It is about Matisse's emotions about art. He felt that both jazz and art allowed a person to improvise and create. To make his collages, Matisse first had his assistants paint white paper with bright colors. Then he cut out shapes without sketching them first. Next he pinned the shapes to his walls and examined them. He moved them around to find the best composition. Finally when he was happy with the arrangement—and this could take years—he glued them to a canvas or board.

Cutout shapes are called **positive** shapes. The holes left in the paper after the shapes have been cut are called **negative** shapes. Matisse used both in his collages.

A **Pierrot** is a sad clown with a white face. Pierrots appeared in shows called pantomimes. Matisse often said the artist was like a Pierrot.

Matisse used only a few colors at a time in his collages.

Matisse liked to **overlap** his shapes. He'd place smaller shapes on top of larger ones, making many layers.

* THERE WERE 370 ORIGINAL COPIES OF JAZZ. THESE ARE ONLY TWO OF THE MANY PLACES TO VIEW IT.

Paul Klee
1879-1940

A drawing is simply a line going for a walk.

Paul Klee loved both music and art. He was born near Bern, Switzerland, and both his parents were musicians. Young Paul was constantly drawing, and he was a master violinist by age 11. This left him with a tough choice. Should he be a painter or a musician when he grew up? He decided on art and studied in Germany, but music always played a large part in his art and life. He played the violin nearly every day until his death.

At age 35, Klee took a two-week trip to Tunisia, a small country in northern Africa. He was blown away by the colors he saw there. He thought the sunlight in Tunisia made the buildings sparkle in a fairytale way. He began experimenting with watercolors, placing blocks of colors next to one another.

Never grow up

Klee loved bright colors and a simple way of painting. He wanted his style to be as free as a child's. Klee liked to doodle. He'd let his pencil move about, then he'd see what he could make out of the shapes and lines that appeared.

Klee was more interested in the feeling the painting gave the viewer than making it look realistic. His people and objects often appear on the canvas as just colors or shapes. His art is called **Abstract Art** because he used simple, abstract shapes.

Klee liked to draw cats, which were his favorite animal.

Anything goes

Klee liked to experiment. He used many different kinds of materials, including chalk, crayon, pastel, spray paint, and ink. Many of his paintings were done on a black or colored background instead of the traditional white. Sometimes he painted on burlap, linen, gauze, cardboard, metal foils, wallpaper, and newsprint.

Back to Switzerland

Klee taught art in Germany at a famous school called the Bauhaus. When the Nazis came into power in the 1930s, his art was **banned**, which means it was not allowed to be shown or viewed. The Nazi government announced that his art was "below standards" and removed it from museum walls. Klee took his family and moved back to Switzerland. Luckily, much of his art was recovered years later.

Senecio

(1922, OIL ON PRIMED GAUZE ON CARDBOARD, KUNSTMUSEUM BASEL IN SWITZERLAND)

This painting is a front-view portrait. *Senecio* means "old man" in Latin. Do you think it looks like an old man? Klee used only simple, geometric shapes. He worked on this painting for many years to get the right combination in his grid of colors. He wanted his painting to have the kind of harmony you hear in music.

How many squares, triangles, and circles can you count?

Klee layered gauze on cardboard and painted over it. In some places, he let the gauze show through.

The palette is of analogous warm colors— red, orange, and yellow. All have had white added to them to give a soft glow. These colors were inspired by Tunisia.

Tissue Paper Face

You Need:

- White paper
- Pencil
- Black crayon
- Colored tissue paper, cut into geometric shapes
- Water
- Foam brush

You Create:

1. Sketch in pencil a large, round head on your white paper. Add a neck, shoulders, and facial features.

2. Outline it in black crayon. Press firmly so the crayon is thick and dark.

3. Dampen your entire paper with your wet foam brush.

4. Place different shapes of tissue paper in a grid pattern all over the paper. Fill up the whole page. Once it is all covered, let it sit for ten minutes. Gently brush the top of the tissue paper with the damp foam brush to get the tissue paper to "bleed."

5. Peel off the tissue paper and throw it away. The tissue paper should leave behind a color pattern on your picture, and the crayon should have "resisted" the color. Let your art dry completely.

Franz Marc
1880-1916

Franz Marc is known for his colorful paintings of animals. He was born in Munich, Germany, and his father was a landscape painter. Marc had a very strict religious childhood and planned to become a priest. By age 20, he had changed his passion to art and attended art school. He moved to Paris and saw the work of Gauguin and Van Gogh. Their use of strong color was eye-opening to him and changed the way he painted.

Four-legged friends

Marc often said he liked animals better than people. He thought animals were smarter and nicer. His approach to painting animals was different from other artists'. He wasn't looking for realism. He said he wanted to paint the animals "from the inside out." He used bright colors to show the animals' souls. Marc did many paintings of horses, and oddly, he was killed while riding a horse at the Battle of Verdun in World War I. A piece of artillery shell hit him in the head.

Blue rider

In 1911, he and the artists Wassily Kandinsky, Alfred Kubin, and Gabriele Münter founded an art group called **Der Blaue Reiter**, which means "The Blue Rider" in German. They saw themselves as spiritual artists galloping forward with new ideas. Other people called their style **Expressionism**, because the artists showed their feelings through their choice of colors and shapes. Marc believed that different colors had different meanings. For example, yellow = gentle and joyous, blue = spiritual, and red = powerful and violent.

Color Code

Franz Marc felt that colors could be joyful, sad, energetic, or lazy. Think of all the phrases we use with color. Can you match them together correctly?

1. Seeing *red*
2. *Green* with envy
3. Feeling *blue*
4. *Yellow* bellied
5. Tickled *pink*
6. A *gray* area

a. Wanting something that someone else has
b. Cowardly, not brave
c. Very happy
d. Very angry
e. Sad
f. Undefined, not one way or another

Answers: 1-d, 2-a, 3-e, 4-b, 5-c, 6-f

Little Blue Horse

(1912, OIL ON CANVAS, SAARLAND MUSEUM IN SAARBRÜCKEN, GERMANY)

There is no question about what the focus of this painting is—the little blue horse, of course! The horse is in the center and stands out against the pink and red landscape. Marc painted the horse blue to show that it was spiritually closer to the sky and heaven than to the earth. He thought that animals were the only creatures worthy of going to heaven.

All the shapes are soft and round.

The curves in the horse are repeated in the hills. Marc thought everything in nature was connected, so he used curvy lines throughout to hold shapes together.

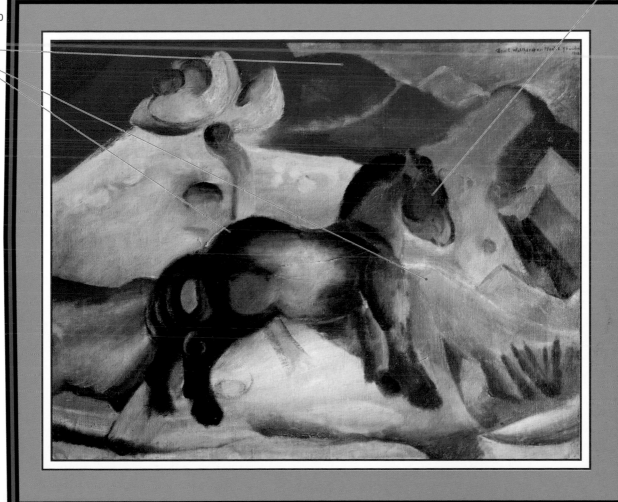

Marc was more interested in capturing the horse's spirit than painting its anatomy correctly.

Children's-book artist Eric Carle wrote and illustrated a book called *The Artist Who Painted a Blue Horse*. Carle hoped to show kids that there is no wrong color in art.

Pablo Picasso
1881-1973

Painting is just another way of keeping a diary.

Pablo Picasso's art has sold for hundreds of millions of dollars all around the world! Born in Málaga, Spain, Picasso began to draw before he could talk. The first word he said was "pencil." He was a restless student and had trouble learning to read and write in school. His father was an art teacher, so he didn't mind that Pablo preferred to concentrate instead on drawing and painting. By 13, young Picasso was a better artist than his father. He headed to art school in Barcelona and then Madrid, but he left both schools because he wanted to create new art in his own way.

Feeling blue . . .
At 23, Picasso moved to Paris, which was the center of the art world. He was very poor. He lived in a shabby studio in a former factory where lots of other artists lived, too. He kept a white mouse as a pet in a table drawer. During this time, he painted very sad scenes and people with long faces in shades of blue. This was called his **Blue Period**.

Pretty in pink
Then Picasso fell in love with a French model and became much happier. His paintings looked happier, too. He painted circuses and mothers and children. They were done in pinks, reds, and oranges. This became known as his **Rose Period**.

A real square
Through Gertrude Stein, an American poet living in Paris, Picasso became good friends with Henri Matisse. Picasso always experimented with new ways of painting, and, with another artist-friend, Georges Braque, he started **Cubism**. Cubists painted objects from many different angles—front, back, top, side—all in the same picture. The Cubists ignored perspective and round shapes, showing the world in a flat, rectangular way. For example, Picasso might put two ears on one side of a face.

Fame and fortune
During his life, Picasso is said to have created more than 20,000 works of art and was famous around the world. There are several museums in Spain and France that show nothing but his work.

Three Musicians

(1921, OIL ON CANVAS, THE MUSEUM OF MODERN ART IN NEW YORK, NEW YORK)

This famous Cubist scene features a Pierrot, a Harlequin, and a monk making music and harmonizing together. The Pierrot wears a blue-and-white suit and plays a clarinet. A Pierrot is a sad clown. In the middle, a Harlequin in an orange-and-yellow patterned suit plays a guitar. A Harlequin is an acrobatic clown. On the right, a monk in a black robe holds sheets of music. Can you find the dog? He's easy to miss. Look beneath the Pierrot. The dog is the same shade of brown as the room.

Everything in the painting is made up of flat shapes. The bright shapes **overlap** and **intersect**, making it hard to tell where one figure stops and another starts.

Picasso fools us into thinking he's created a cut-paper collage, but it's really an oil painting.

Found Objects

Picasso didn't just use paint on his canvases. He often stuck pieces of newspaper, musical scores, and wallpaper to his paintings. He even attached spoons or wood to make them 3-D. When artists use such random things in their art, they're called "found objects" because you might find them lying around the house. Contemporary artists have used trash in their art. What can you find in your house to use?

Gertrude Stein called this painting a "still life." Do you agree?

Salvador Dalí
1904-1989

Strange, weird, wacky, and bizarre are all words used to describe Salvador Dalí—and Dalí was often the one using them! He was happiest when he was shocking people with both his art and his behavior. Born in Figueras, Spain, Dalí experimented with many different art styles as a child. He painted landscapes. He painted portraits. He tried Impressionism and Cubism. In art school in Madrid, Dalí hung out with troublemakers. He told the teachers that he was a better artist than they were and refused to listen to them. They kicked him out, but he kept on painting and experimenting.

Dreamlike and absurd

Soon Dalí discovered a style of art called **Surrealism**. Surrealism means "above realism." Surrealism is a wacky, sideways view of life that often pokes fun at the world. Surrealists feel that dreams, not rational thoughts, show what's truly hidden in our minds. Dalí described his work as "hand-painted dream photographs." Surreal art places ordinary people and everyday objects in bizarre surroundings. For example, Dalí once attached a lobster to a telephone!

Wacky guy

Dalí was quite weird. He refused to let anyone see his bare feet. He wouldn't walk on grass because he had an intense fear of grasshoppers. He would jump up and down in public to get attention.

Surreal Collage

Let your imagination run wild as you make your own surreal art!

You Need:
- Paper
- Markers
- Glue stick
- Magazines
- Scissors

You Create:

1. Cut out random objects from magazines. Find images that are strange. Also find everyday objects, such as toothpaste, a bicycle, a dog, or a roll of toilet paper. Take your time cutting out the pictures so the edges are clean and precise.

2. Next, cut out a landscape background and glue it to the paper. Or draw your own landscape with markers.

3. Choose images from your pile that work in **juxtaposition**, which means they don't normally go together but are now placed next to each other. For example, using a country lane background, glue a picture of a fish riding a bicycle and balancing a pear on the handlebars. Now you are making surreal art!

The Persistence of Memory

(1931, OIL ON CANVAS, MUSEUM OF MODERN ART IN NEW YORK, NEW YORK)

This desert landscape covered with melting watches is the most famous Surrealist painting.
Dalí said part of the idea came to him in a dream. Why do you think he shows time melting?
Many people feel Dalí is telling us that time is meaningless.

The landscape is of northeastern Spain, where Dalí spent his childhood.

Three melting watches are all stopped at different times.

The fly on the watch and the ants symbolize decay, as if time is losing its meaning.

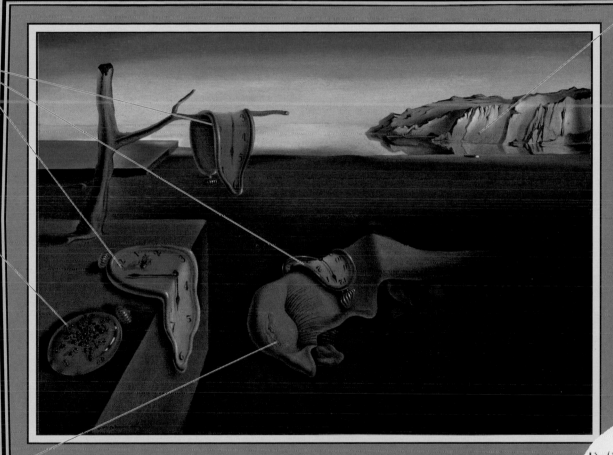

In all of his paintings, you can find Dalí's self-portrait. Here he is!

Dalí had an extraordinary mustache that he liked to shape into whiskers, a figure eight, and handlebars!

The True Cheese Story

Dalí spent the day painting in his studio. His picture showed a beach and the rocky coastline by the sea. He had painted an olive tree with most of the branches missing. The rest of the painting was empty. He didn't know how to fill it. That evening, he was tired and had a headache. He told his friends and wife to go the movies without him. He sat at his dinner table for a long time, staring at the leftover Camembert cheese. Camembert is a soft, round, gooey cheese. Then he had an idea! He went to his studio and filled the painting with clocks that looked like melting Camembert cheeses. When his wife returned from the movies, he showed her the painting and asked if she thought she'd forget it in three years' time. She felt that once someone had seen the image there was no way he or she would ever forget it.

Jackson Pollock
1912-1956

Love it or hate it, Jackson Pollock changed the way we look at art. From the moment of his birth in Cody, Wyoming, Pollock was full of energy. A restless kid who didn't like to follow the rules, Pollack's mother encouraged him to paint. Until World War II, Paris had been the center of the art world. Now it was New York. At age 18, Pollock moved to New York City and enrolled in the Art Students League.

Pollock started out doing realistic drawings. He was fascinated by the Surrealists and the idea that art should just flow from the mind of the artist. His goal was to paint his emotions, letting them come out without his thoughts blocking their way. When he painted, he tried to make his mind blank.

Drip, drip, splat

Pollock became famous for his "**drip**" or "splatter" paintings. They are also known as "**action paintings**." In his farmhouse in East Hampton, New York, he laid huge canvases flat on the barn floor. He'd move around, approaching the painting from every angle. He dripped, splashed, and threw paint directly from the paint can. Pollock used his whole body—flinging his arms and moving his weight back and forth. The lines of paint followed the dancing of his body. He never stopped moving while he worked, which earned him the nickname "**Action Jackson**."

> On the floor I am more at ease. I feel nearer, more a part of the painting, since this way I can walk around it, work from the four sides and literally be in the painting.

A little of this, a little of that

To apply the paint to the canvas, Pollock used anything he could find, including sticks, knives, rods, and turkey basters. He never wanted to see any brushstrokes. Sometimes he sprinkled sand, pieces of glass, screws, or ashes from his cigarettes on the canvas to give his work texture. To build up layer after layer, he used industrial or enamel paint, which dried quickly.

Emotions in motion

Pollock didn't plan out or sketch his paintings first. He let his emotions guide his hand and body. Pollock insisted that every line, drip, and dribble was controlled. This style of abstract painting is called **Abstract Expressionism**.

Number 1A, 1948

(1948, OIL AND ENAMEL PAINT ON CANVAS, THE MUSEUM OF MODERN ART IN NEW YORK, NEW YORK)

As with all his drip paintings, this one has no recognizable subject. Pollock stopped giving his paintings titles and numbered them instead. He said numbers didn't make the viewer think about anything before experiencing the painting.

Splatter!

Channel your inner Pollock in this fun yet messy art project.

You Need:

- Canvas board
- Acrylic or tempera paint, watered down
- Paintbrushes, popsicle sticks, toothbrushes, plastic forks, turkey basters
- Plastic tarp or disposable tablecloth (the bigger the better)
- Old clothes

You Create:

1. It's best to work outside. Lay out your tarp and place pots of watered-down paint and your canvas on top of it.

2. Wearing old clothes, dip your painting tool into the paint and fling, splatter, flick, or drip it on your canvas. Do not paint!

3. Change position. Move around. Stop if your painting begins to look muddy—you want to see the fabulous swirls and splatters.

On the upper right, you can see where he left a handprint. His handprint was his signature.

The layered ribbons of paint create an intricate web. It looks messy, but there is a balance and a rhythm.

Pollock once tore down a wall in his studio to fit in a massive 20-foot canvas.

Jacob Lawrence
1917-2000

Jacob Lawrence was one of the most influential African American artists. When he was born, his parents had recently relocated to Atlantic City, New Jersey, from the South. When he was 13, he moved to a part of New York City called Harlem with his mother, brother, and sister. His mother enrolled him in an after-school program at a community youth center. There, Jacob first experimented with art using crayons and scraps of paper. Later, at home, he painted scenes on used cardboard boxes. He would cut one side off the box to give his scenes a 3-D effect.

Lawrence liked to visit art museums and read art books. He wondered why there was so little about African Americans in the art he saw. He felt that if people didn't see themselves or their history reflected in a painting, then they couldn't be proud of themselves or their ancestors. He vowed to change that.

> *When the subject is strong, simplicity is the only way to treat it.*

African American Artists

For a long time, art history failed to showcase the talent of African American artists due to centuries of discrimination. While it is impossible to squeeze every important name into this small space, here are some African American artists you may want to learn more about: portrait painter **Joshua Johnson**; landscape painter **Robert S. Duncanson**; Realist painter **Henry Ossawa Tanner**; abstract painter **Alma Thomas**; Harlem Renaissance artists **William H. Johnson**, **Palmer Hayden**, **Malvin Gray Johnson**, **Sargent Johnson**, and **Augusta Savage**; collage artist **Romare Bearden**; Black Arts Movement artists **Jeff Donaldson** and **Betye Saar**, and contemporary silhouette artist **Kara Walker**.

Telling stories

Lawrence went to art school, then became a teacher and held many other jobs. He saved his money to do what he loved—paint! While living in an old building in New York City with no heat or running water, he painted a series of 60 paintings called *The Migration Series*. This series tells the story of how two million African Americans from the rural South traveled to the urban North during and after World War I, looking for jobs, better conditions, and a life without discrimination. The Great Migration, as it was called, was the largest group of people to move from one part of the United States to another, and it brought change to America.

Dynamic cubism

Over one year, Lawrence painted all 60 panels at once, color by color, so they all shared the same palette. Lawrence used bright colors and a flat composition. Simple shapes created the heads and bodies. He called his modern style **Dynamic Cubism**.

Breaking barriers

At the age of 24, Lawrence became the first African American artist to have a painting included in the permanent collection of the Museum of Modern Art in New York City. Today, his work is in more than 200 museums.

Lawrence said, "To me, migration means movement. . . . I tried to convey this rhythm in the pictures."

The Migration of the Negro, no. 12

(1940-41, TEMPERA ON HARDBOARD, THE MUSEUM OF MODERN ART IN NEW YORK, NEW YORK)

This painting is panel number 12 in Lawrence's *Migration Series*. In the early 1900s, many African Americans had to travel far from home to find work in the factories in the North. Lawrence captures the difficulty of the journey and their struggles and hopes. In this panel, people wait in a crowded train station. There were no airports then. The railroad was the link from South to North. Each picture has a number and is meant to be viewed in order to tell a historical story. Each picture also has a caption. The caption for number 12 is: "The railroad stations were at times so over-packed with people leaving that special guards had to be called in to keep order."

Lawrence His flattened, angular forms show the influence of Cubism.

Lawrence saw his series of 60 paintings as a single work. He was upset when the Museum of Modern Art in New York bought only the even-numbered ones, and the Phillips Collection in Washington, D.C., bought only the odd-numbered ones.

Andy Warhol
1928-1987

Don't think about making art, just get it done. Let everyone else decide if it's good or bad, whether they love it or hate it. While they are deciding, make even more art.

Andy Warhol was the rock star of the art world. He created **Pop Art**, one of the most fun styles in modern art. Born in Pittsburgh, Pennsylvania, Warhol was a sickly child who was kept home from school a lot. His mother promised that every time he finished a coloring book page, she'd reward him with a chocolate bar. Young Andy did *a lot* of coloring! He also read a lot of movie magazines and dreamed about being famous one day.

As a boy, Warhol took weekend art classes at a nearby museum. After graduating college with a degree in art, he moved to New York City to start his career in advertising and fashion illustration. One of his first jobs was illustrating shoes for *Glamour* magazine. His real name was Andy Warhola, but when *Glamour* printed his illustrations, they left off the final "a" by mistake. He decided to keep it that way.

Art party

Andy loved drawing colorful shoes—and he got many shoe-drawing jobs. He also designed greeting cards, album covers, and department store windows. He became so busy that he'd invite his friends to his apartment to help color in his work. Even his mom helped! Warhol was very successful, but he wanted to do something new with his art. And he wanted to be famous.

Art is everywhere

Looking at other artists, Warhol felt that Abstract Expressionism was too self-centered—who cared what some artist was feeling? Instead, he showed that art could be found in the signs, advertisements, and packaging all around us. He made pictures of dollar bills, Coca-Cola bottles, and soup cans. This art became known as Pop Art because it was based on popular culture.

When he first showed the soup-can paintings in a Los Angeles gallery when he was 34, people were angry and said it was an advertisement, not real art. Warhol fought back, and asked, "Why isn't it art?" Warhol explained that he painted objects that we see every day but don't stop to think about. He believed that "everything is beautiful." He made sure to copy the can's packaging exactly. He didn't want to bring his emotions into his art.

Every month, Warhol placed an opened cardboard box by his desk and tossed in photographs, letters, movie-ticket stubs, souvenirs, or whatever else caught his interest. Then he'd store it away. He called his boxes "time capsules." By the time he died, he'd filled 612 boxes.

Fame!

Warhol became a legend while alive—and that was his plan from the beginning. Early on, he decided that looking bizarre would make people remember him and lead to sales. His trademark look included large sunglasses, a black leather jacket, high-heeled boots, a white wig, and pale skin. He owned over 400 wigs! "In the future, everyone will be famous for 15 minutes," Warhol promised. He was famous for a lot longer.

Warhol printed bold, graphic images on a white background so the soup can stood out. He wanted the can to appear valuable.

The Factory

The Factory was Warhol's famous art workshop in New York City. The large building used to be a hat factory. He painted all the brick walls silver and covered the concrete in tinfoil. He even wore a silver wig. Here, Warhol was able to produce a lot of pictures with the help of a lot of people, as if he truly worked in a factory. "I want to be like a machine," he said. His assistants were similar to the apprentices who worked with famous artists hundreds of years ago.

Warhol made movies at the Factory, too. In the movies, he had the "actors" simply be themselves rather than act a part. He made a movie called *Sleep* that showed a man sleeping for six hours! The Factory was not only for making art. Warhol had large parties with lots of famous guests, and it became one of the coolest places to hang out in the city.

Campbell's Soup Cans
(1962, SILKSCREEN, THE MUSEUM OF MODERN ART IN NEW YORK, NEW YORK)

Nothing says ordinary like a can of Campbell's soup. In the 1960s, the red-and-white label was in every grocery store and in every pantry. Warhol did a **series** of the soup cans, painting each of Campbell's 32 varieties. Each work in the series is a photo **silkscreen** print. Silkscreen was used most often to make advertising posters, because it allowed many, many copies to be made of one image. To Warhol, this method helped show how soup cans are all around us, and that there was beauty in everyday objects.

Silkscreen is a way to print many colors. A screen of fine silk mesh is pulled across and secured to a frame. A stencil of a design is attached to the screen. Ink is then pressed through the cut-out area with a special sponge called a squeegee.

After World War II, colors became brighter and design became more graphic. Andy Warhol was the king of Pop Art, but other artists, such as **Jasper Johns** and **Yayoi Kusana**, joined him in this style. **Roy Lichtenstein** was famous for art that looked like comic strips.

After Pop, some art became super simple. Many artists painted with only one or two colors, or their canvases showed just a block of color. These **Minimalist** artists included **Mark Rothko**, **Frank Stella**, and **Robert Rauschenberg**.

Photography was a popular form of art. **Ansel Adams** was known for his striking black-and-white photos. **David Hockney** combined photography with Pop Art. **Photorealism** took hold in the 1970s. Artists such as **Chuck Close** used photographs instead of models and then painted them in sharp detail. **Cindy Sherman** photographed herself in a variety of wigs and costumes. More recently, the ability to morph photos on the computer has allowed artists such as **Gerhard Richter** to create amazing works by painting over his photos.

Art grew a lot bigger in size. **Diego Rivera** was famous for his murals showing Mexican history, and the Brazilian twins **Os Gemeos** are known today for their large, colorful graffiti murals. **Graffiti** comes from an Italian word meaning "to scratch." Graffiti spray-painted on buildings is a crime, but artists such as **Cy Twombly** and **Jean-Michel Basquiat** made graffiti on canvases into art.

th Art Now?

Sculpture is no longer only clay, marble, and bronze. Today, recycled materials, fabrics, gems, and steel are used. **Jeff Koons** created a steel sculpture that looks like an enormous balloon dog. **Damien Hirst** covered a skull in diamonds!

Art is also used to express political messages. **Shepard Fairey's** graphic *Hope* poster for President Barack Obama's 2008 election campaign was displayed everywhere. Chinese artist **Ai Wei Wei** uses his art to show the injustice of his government.

As you can see, art is constantly changing. There are no rules. Anything can be art and anyone can make art. This includes you! Go ahead and be creative. You never know, someday your art may appear in a book like this one.

Index

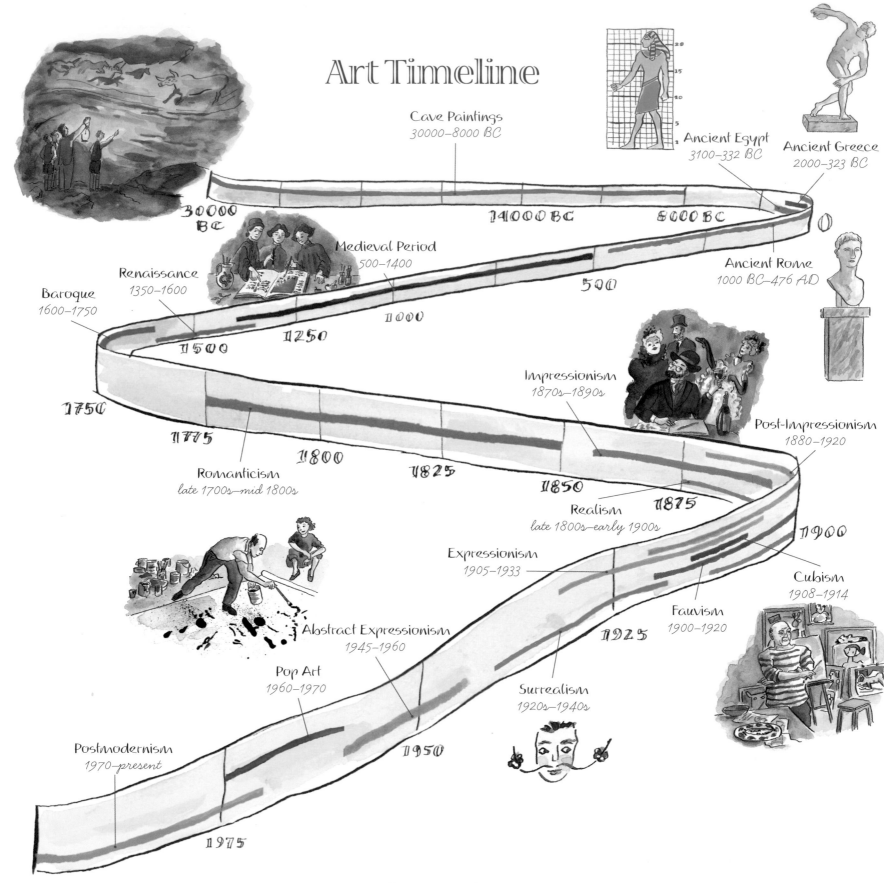

Art Timeline

Cave Paintings
30000–8000 BC

Ancient Egypt
3100–332 BC

Ancient Greece
2000–323 BC

30000 BC

14000 BC

8000 BC

0

Ancient Rome
1000 BC–476 AD

Medieval Period
500–1400

Renaissance
1350–1600

Baroque
1600–1750

1500

1250

1000

500

Impressionism
1870s–1890s

Post-Impressionism
1880–1920

1750

1775

1800

1825

1850

1875

1900

Romanticism
late 1700s–mid 1800s

Realism
late 1800s–early 1900s

Expressionism
1905–1933

Cubism
1908–1914

Fauvism
1900–1920

Abstract Expressionism
1945–1960

1925

Pop Art
1960–1970

Surrealism
1920s–1940s

1950

Postmodernism
1970–present

1975

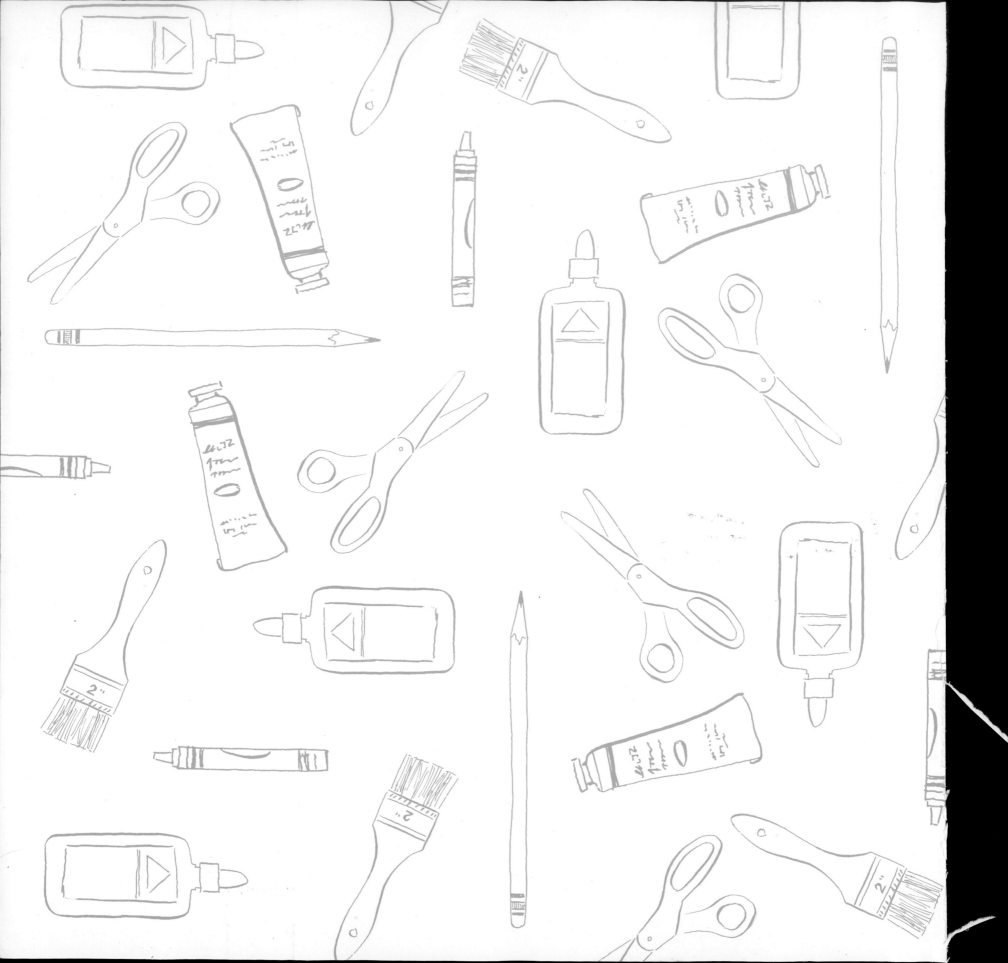